FORMED IN C

ABOUT THE SERIES

Who is Jesus Christ? What does it mean to know him? What do the Church and her sacraments have to do with him? How are we to follow him?

These are the questions at the heart of the Catholic faith, and these are the questions the Formed in Christ series answers. Rooted in the story of Salvation History and steeped in the writings of the Fathers and Doctors of the Church, this series of high school textbooks from the St. Paul Center seeks to engage minds and hearts as it presents the tenets of the Catholic faith in Scripture and Tradition.

Over the course of this comprehensive, four-year curriculum, students will learn the fundamentals of Church teaching on the Person and mission of Jesus Christ, Sacred Scripture, the Church, the sacraments, morality, Church history, vocations, Catholic social teaching, and more. Just as important, they'll be invited, again and again, to enter more deeply into a relationship with Christ, growing in love of him as they grow in knowledge of him.

PUBLISHED

Evidence of Things Unseen: An Introduction to Fundamental Theology
Andrew Willard Jones and Louis St. Hilaire.
Edited by Stimpson Chapman

The Word Became Flesh: An Introduction to Christology
Andrew Willard Jones. Edited by Emily Stimpson Chapman

That You Might Have Life: An Introduction to the Paschal Mystery of Christ
Louis St. Hilaire. Edited by Emily Stimpson Chapman

I Will Build My Church: An Introduction to Ecclesiology
Andrew Willard Jones. Edited by Emily Stimpson Chapman

Do This in Remembrance: An Introduction to the Sacraments
Jacob Wood. Edited by Emily Stimpson Chapman

Christ Alive in Us: An Introduction to Moral Theology
John Meinert and Emily Stimpson Chapman

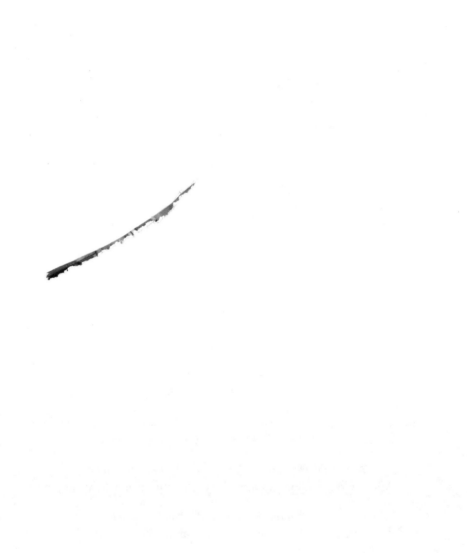

CHRIST ALIVE IN US

AN INTRODUCTION TO MORAL THEOLOGY

CHRIST ALIVE IN US

AN INTRODUCTION TO
MORAL THEOLOGY

JOHN MEINERT AND
EMILY STIMPSON CHAPMAN

EMMAUS
ROAD
PUBLISHING

www.emmausroad.org
Steubenville, Ohio

In Grateful Recognition of Lawrence Joseph & Lynn Marie Blanford

Emmaus Road Publishing
1468 Parkview Circle
Steubenville, Ohio 43952

Library of Congress Control Number: 2019934890

ISBN 978-1-949013-50-4

Cover image: *Christ and the Woman of Samaria*, William Hamilton (1751–1801)

Series design by Margaret Ryland

Cover and layout by Emily Feldkamp

TABLE OF CONTENTS

Part I

Joy and Blessing:

God's Plan for Our Life in Christ

Is Catholic moral teaching one big "No?"

Many people think so. They hear the Church saying no to premarital sex, no to abortion, no to same-sex marriage, no to unjust wages, no to drunkenness—in short, no to many of the things they want to do—and assume that the Church exists as some kind of moral traffic cop. They think of her, in effect, as the Fun Police, as someone who's there to make sure nobody enjoys themselves too much.

Those people, however, couldn't be more wrong. In the Gospel of John, Jesus Christ sums up his mission on earth in one sentence: "I came that they may have life, and have it abundantly" (John 10:10). This sentence informs the whole of Catholic moral teaching, which isn't one big no, but rather one big yes. It is a yes to Jesus Christ, a yes to God's plan, a yes to real love, and a yes to real joy.

God created us and redeemed us so that we can have life in abundance—not just in heaven, but even now, on earth. By his providence, he calls all people to experience perfect happiness and, through his Church, he gives us the guidance we need to get there (CCC 302). Catholic moral theology is that guidance. Far from negating what is authentically human, it radically affirms all that is good and true. It is the study of how we can have happy lives, both now and forever.

To study moral theology is to discover who we are and for what we are made. It's an encounter with the God who loves us, and it's an essential part of our quest for meaning, fulfillment, and happiness. This book aims to assist you in that quest in four ways.

First, it seeks to help you understand God's call to you—his call to live the fullness of life in Jesus Christ. Second, it seeks to help you know God's plan for you—the guidance he offers you in the Old Testament, the New Testament, and the life of the Church—for living life in Christ. Third, it seeks to help you understand the nature of sin—of the various ways we can separate ourselves from God. And fourth, this book seeks to help you know and take advantage of all the various types of help and spiritual assistance God offers you to avoid sin and live a life of grace in Jesus Christ.

Ultimately, though, the goal of this book is simple: it seeks to help you say yes to all the love, joy, and life God desires for you. It seeks to help you say yes to perfect happiness.

Chapter 1

THE DESIRE OF OUR HEARTS

We hear the call to perfect happiness first and foremost in our hearts. Each of us desires joy. We desire love, satisfaction, and fulfilment. None of us want to be unhappy. None of us want to be unloved. None of us want to be alone. No matter how much we've been hurt, deep down we all desire someone who sees us, knows us, and loves us. We also desire to do something meaningful, something that gives our life purpose and direction. We want to matter. We want to feel that our lives are worth something.

Unfortunately, we often seek to fulfill those desires in the wrong way. We entrust our hearts to new friends or a new dating relationship, only to find ourselves disappointed and rejected. Or, we think success will get us the fulfillment and love we want, so we pour our energy into school, sports, work, even good deeds . . . only to find, sooner or later, that it's not enough. We still long for more—more meaning, more success, more love.

There is a reason for this—a reason why there always seems to be a hole in the human heart that nothing can satisfy, or at least not satisfy for long. The Catechism of the Catholic Church explains:

> The desire for God is written in the human heart, because man is created by God and for God; and God never ceases to draw man to himself. Only in God will he find the truth and happiness he never stops searching for. (CCC 27)

In other words, God is the one for whom we long. God is the one for whom we were made. The hole in our hearts is a God-shaped hole. It is made to be filled by his infinite love, and nothing short of his infinite love can fill it. Which is why, when we seek meaning, purpose, and happiness outside of God, the hole remains. Nothing in this world can ultimately satisfy our hearts, because our hearts weren't made for this world; they were made for heaven. They were made for God.

The Nature of the Human Person

|| **ASSIGNED READING**
|| Genesis 1:26–28

The call to happiness that we hear first in our hearts is made clear to us through Revelation. Starting with the Book of Genesis, the Word of God explains to us who we are and how we must live if we want to find the love and happiness we so deeply desire.

Despite what some people think, the opening chapters of the Bible are not a lesson in science; they are a lesson in fundamental truths about God, the human person, and creation. And the most important of those truths is this: from the beginning, God created man and woman to exist in loving communion with him. That is to say, he created us for eternal friendship with himself, wanting us to not only know him and love him in this life, but to know him and love him forever, in eternity, in heaven:

> For God so loved the world that he gave his only-begotten Son, that whoever believes in him should not perish but have eternal life. (John 3:16)

This friendship between the human person and God is unique. No other creature can enjoy such a friendship because only the human person was made "in the image of God" (Gen 1:26). This means only the human person possesses a rational soul. Of all material creation, the human person, and the human person alone, possesses an intellect and a free will (CCC 1951). The intellect allows us, like God, to know the truth, and the will allows us, like God, to love the good.

> Being in the image of God the human individual possesses the dignity of a person, who is not just something, but someone. He is capable of self-knowledge, of self-possession and of freely giving himself and entering into communion with other persons. (CCC 357)

St. Thomas Aquinas described the image of God in three ways. The first is our "natural aptitude to know and love God"[1] and is based on our soul's rationality. Our resemblance to God in this way cannot increase, decrease, or change. We cannot gain it or lose it. It abides in us as long as we abide. It is present even when we are not exercising our rationality or not exercising it well. It doesn't matter if we're sleeping. It doesn't matter if we're sinning. All that matters is that we are human. All people image God, whether we are a hardened criminal, a comatose hospital patient, or an unborn child. It is "intrinsic" to who we are (CCC 1944). Likewise, all people, whether we are good or bad, have value because we are made in the image of God. All people are precious simply by the fact that we exist.

Our rational soul gives us another power: the power to choose. Our intellect enables us to know the truth and our will enables us to love the good, but neither forces us to choose the good. We are free—free to embrace truth or reject truth, free to love or not love, free to accept God's call to friendship or reject God's call to friendship. As the Catechism puts it, man is "called by grace to a covenant with his Creator, to offer him a response of faith and love that no other creature can give in his stead" (CCC 357).

Through this freedom, rightly exercised, St. Augustine (354–430) says that the image of God is perfected in us. Or, as St. Thomas Aquinas explained, our freedom makes it possible for us to image God not just in a static, unchanging way, but also in a dynamic changing way.[2] By this,

---

[1] Thomas Aquinas, *Summa Theologica* (hereafter cited as ST) I, q. 93, a. 4, co.
[2] Aquinas, ST I, q. 93, a. 4, co.

St. Thomas meant that if we choose to receive the grace he offers us and to love God, we can image God even more perfectly. We can become more like him. We know more as he knows and love more as he loves, and eventually enjoy perfect friendship—"eternal beatitude"—with him in heaven.

Again, though, this increase in perfection requires something from us. It requires our consent, our *fiat*, our yes to God's call. And that yes isn't always easy to give.

SELECTED READING
Second Vatican Council, Pastoral Constitution on the Church in the Modern World *Gaudium et Spes* (December 7, 1965), nos. 8–10

Within the individual person there develops rather frequently an imbalance between an intellect which is modern in practical matters and a theoretical system of thought which can neither master the sum total of its ideas, nor arrange them adequately into a synthesis. Likewise an imbalance arises between a concern for practicality and efficiency, and the demands of moral conscience; also very often between the conditions of collective existence and the requisites of personal thought, and even of contemplation. At length there develops an imbalance between specialized human activity and a comprehensive view of reality.

As for the family, discord results from population, economic and social pressures, or from difficulties which arise between succeeding generations, or from new social relationships between men and women.

Differences crop up too between races and between various kinds of social orders; between wealthy nations and those which are less influential or are needy; finally, between international institutions born of the popular desire for peace, and the ambition to propagate one's own ideology, as well as collective greeds existing in nations or other groups.

What results is mutual distrust, enmities, conflicts and hardships. Of such is man at once the cause and the victim.

Meanwhile the conviction grows not only that humanity can and should increasingly consolidate its control over creation, but even more, that it devolves on humanity to establish a political, social and economic order which will growingly serve man and help individuals as well as groups to affirm and develop the dignity proper to them.

As a result many persons are quite aggressively demanding those benefits of which with vivid awareness they judge themselves to be deprived either through injustice or unequal distribution. Nations on the road to progress, like those recently made independent, desire to participate in the goods of modern civilization, not only in the political field but also economically, and to play their part freely on the world scene. Still they continually fall behind while very often their economic and other dependence on wealthier nations advances more rapidly.

People hounded by hunger call upon those better off. Where they have not yet won it, women claim for themselves an equity with men before the law and in fact. Laborers and farmers seek not only to provide for the necessities of life, but to develop the gifts of their personality by their labors and indeed to take part in regulating economic, social, political and cultural life. Now, for the first time in human history all people are convinced that the benefits of culture ought to be and actually can be extended to everyone.

Still, beneath all these demands lies a deeper and more widespread longing: persons and societies thirst for a full and free life worthy of man; one in which they can subject to their own welfare all that the modern world can offer them so abundantly. In addition, nations try harder every day to bring about a kind of universal community.

Since all these things are so, the modern world shows itself at once powerful and weak, capable of the noblest deeds or the foulest; before it lies the path to freedom or to slavery, to progress or retreat, to brotherhood or hatred. Moreover, man is becoming aware that it is his responsibility to guide aright the forces which he has unleashed and which can enslave him or minister to him. That is why he is putting questions to himself.

The truth is that the imbalances under which the modern world labors are linked with that more basic imbalance which is rooted in the heart of man. For in man himself many elements wrestle with one another. Thus, on the one hand, as a creature he experiences his limitations in a multitude of ways; on the other he feels himself to be boundless in his desires and summoned to a higher life. Pulled by manifold attractions he is constantly forced to choose among them and renounce some. Indeed, as a weak and sinful being, he often does what he would not, and fails to do what he would. Hence he suffers from internal divisions, and from these flow so many and such great discords in society. No doubt many whose lives are infected with a practical materialism are blinded against any sharp insight into this kind of dramatic situation; or else, weighed down by unhappiness they are prevented from giving the matter any thought. Thinking they have found serenity in an interpretation of reality everywhere proposed these days, many look forward to a genuine and total emancipation of humanity wrought solely by human effort; they are convinced that the future rule of man over the earth will satisfy every desire of his heart. Nor are there lacking men who despair of any meaning to life and praise the boldness of those who think that human existence is devoid of any inherent significance and strive to confer a total meaning on it by their own ingenuity alone.

Nevertheless, in the face of the modern development of the world, the number constantly swells of the people who raise the most basic questions or recognize them with a new sharpness: what is man? What is this sense of sorrow, of evil, of death, which continues to exist despite so much progress? What purpose have these victories purchased at so high a cost? What can man offer to society, what can he expect from it? What follows this earthly life?

The Church firmly believes that Christ, who died and was raised up for all, can through His Spirit offer man the light and the strength to measure up to his supreme destiny. Nor has any other name under the heaven been given to man by which it is fitting for him to be saved. She likewise holds that in her most benign Lord and Master can be found the key, the focal point and the goal of man, as well as of all human history. The Church also maintains that beneath all changes there are many realities which do not change and which have their ultimate foundation in Christ, Who is the same yesterday and today, yes and forever. Hence under the light of Christ, the image of the unseen God, the firstborn of every creature, the council wishes to speak to all men in order to shed light on the mystery of man and to cooperate in finding the solution to the outstanding problems of our time.

QUESTIONS FOR REVIEW

1. Why is the desire for God written on the human heart?
2. About what do the opening chapters of the Book of Genesis aim to teach us?
3. For what did God create us?
4. What does it mean to be made "in the image of God"?
5. What makes it possible for God's image to be perfected in us?

QUESTIONS FOR DISCUSSION

1. What is your deepest and greatest desire in life?
2. Have you ever gotten the very thing you wanted in life only to eventually be disappointed by it? Describe what happened.
3. Describe a time when you freely chose to do something good. How did this shape you as a person? Describe a time you freely chose to do something wrong. How did that shape you as a person?

Chapter 2

Our Need for God's Help and Guidance

Original Innocence

|| ASSIGNED READING
|| Genesis 2

On the one hand, it makes no sense. If the God of the universe is offering us eternal joy and friendship with him, why would we say no? Why would anyone say no? But our own experience shows us all too clearly that, at some point, we do say no. In one way or another, every single one of us rejects God's offer of friendship and grace through sin, which is failing to love him, ourselves, and others as we should. The reason for this failure of ours is also given to us in the Book of Genesis.

There, we see the first man and the first woman—Adam and Eve—living as God called them to live: in harmony with each other and creation. Both the man and the woman are made in the image of God, equal in dignity, yet different. This difference reflects God's design for creation. Says the Catechism, "God created man and woman *together* and willed each *for* the other" (CCC 371, emphasis added). As man and wife, Adam and Eve saw each other, knew each other, and loved each other. There was no lust, no envy, no desire to use the other or harm the other. They were, the Bible tells us, "naked, and were not ashamed" (Gen 2:25).

The same harmony that existed between man and woman in the beginning also existed between humanity and the rest of creation. God had given our first parents the command to "Be fruitful and multiply, and fill the earth and subdue it" (Gen 1:28), which made Adam and Eve God's stewards. They shared responsibility for the world and cared for the world—a world that was not theirs, but God's (Gen 1:31). In turn, creation didn't pose a threat to them, but rather provided for their needs.

On another level, God provided even more completely for Adam and Eve's needs; and they knew it. God, Genesis tells us, ordered all things by his will (Gen 1:1) and walked in the garden, meaning he knew Adam and Eve as intimate friends or as his children (3:8). There was no distance between them. The harmony that existed between man and woman, and human beings and creation, existed also between human beings and God.

This time of harmony—between man and woman, humanity and creation, and humanity and God—is called Original Innocence. Likewise, Adam and Eve's state of holiness and justice is called Original Justice. The Catechism describes this state in these words:

> By the radiance of this grace all dimensions of man's life were confirmed. As long as he remained in the divine intimacy, man would not have to suffer or die [Cf. Gen 2:17; 3:16, 19]. The inner harmony of the human person, the harmony between man and woman [Cf. Gen 2:25], and finally the harmony between the first couple and all creation, comprised the state called "original justice." (CCC 376)

Because of this state, Adam and Eve did not have to suffer or die, and work was not a burden. Doing God's will came easily and naturally to them. Their intellects readily knew the truth, and their wills readily loved the good. For a time, they chose to say yes to God and enjoyed intimate friendship with him.

Then, one day, they chose differently.

The Fall

|| ASSIGNED READING
|| Genesis 3:1–6

In the Book of Genesis, God tells Adam and Eve that, as stewards of creation, they are free to eat of every tree in the Garden, save for one: the tree of the knowledge of good and evil. This tree represents God's dominion over what is right and wrong—his understanding of what will make human beings happy (the good) and what will make them unhappy (evil) (CCC 396). Every second that Adam and Eve chose not to eat the fruit of that tree, they choose happiness; they choose good; they choose to let the image of God be perfected within them.

When Satan enters the garden in the form of a serpent, however, and convinces them to eat from the tree of the knowledge of good and evil, Adam and Eve reject the good. They choose what is bad for them—what is evil—and lose not only communion with God, but also with each other and the natural world.

It's easy to dismiss these chapters in the Bible as a fairy tale, but the Church doesn't. She takes them seriously, if not literally, recognizing, as the Catechism explains, that:

> The account of the fall in *Genesis* 3 uses figurative language, but affirms a primeval event, a deed that took place *at the beginning of the history of man* [Cf. GS 13 § 1]. Revelation gives us the certainty of faith that the whole of human history is marked by the original fault freely committed by our first parents [Cf. Council of Trent: DS 1513; Pius XII: DS 3897; Paul VI: AAS 58 (1966), 654]. (CCC 390)

Through the account of Adam and Eve's fall, God shows us that at the very beginning of human history, our first parents were tempted by Satan and made a profoundly bad choice. They rejected God by rejecting the good. They also rejected their own creaturely nature, attempting to become, in a sense, gods in their own right, determining for themselves "good and evil," without any reference to God himself (Gen 3:5).

Suffering the Consequences

|| ASSIGNED READING
|| Genesis 3:7–24

With that rejection, with that choice, our first parents lost the grace of original justice—the grace by which they were properly ordered to God, each other, and the natural world.

First, their relationship with God became broken and clouded; they hid from God when he came to them in the garden, and then, as part of their punishment, they had to go east of Eden, which means away from God's presence (Gen 3:24).

Second, their relationship with each other was broken. Power and lust entered into the relationship of man and woman. "Your desire shall be for your husband," the Lord told Eve in Genesis 3:16, "and he shall rule over you."

Finally, man and woman's relationship with the natural world was broken. Work became hard. Caring for the world became a challenge. And the earth no longer easily and readily provided for humanity's needs.

With sin, sickness and death also came into the world. "You are dust, and to dust you shall return," God told Adam (Gen 3:19). Another kind of death came as well: spiritual death. Actually, it came first. As soon as Adam and Eve rejected God, they lost sanctifying grace, the life of God that he had breathed into them at creation (Gen 2:7). From that point on, Adam and Eve didn't stop imaging God but it became harder to act in accord with that dignity. It became harder to know the truth and choose the good. Their intellects were now darkened, and their wills weakened (CCC 399–400).

Inheriting the Consequences

Adam and Eve suffered the consequences of their sin for the rest of their lives. And so do we. We, too, suffer the consequences of their sin, of original sin. Every human being is now born with the same darkened intellect and weakened will. So, we desire the truth, but find it hard to know the truth. We desire the good, but find it hard to do the good. We also, at times, don't desire the true good and instead desire to do what is bad. The Church describes this tendency as "concupiscence," which essentially means "a tendency to sin."

The consequences of Adam and Eve's sin go beyond concupiscence, though. Also, like Adam and Eve, our relationships with members of the opposite sex are now often marred by lust and domination. Likewise, we all die. We all suffer. We all must exist in a world where natural disasters, plagues, and dangers from the animal world threaten us (CCC 400).

Most difficult of all, every single person is born into the world without the life of God in our souls, without sanctifying grace. This is the essence of the Church's teaching on original sin:

> Although it is proper to each individual [Cf. Council of Trent: DS 1513], original sin does not have the character of a personal fault in any of Adam's descendants. It is a deprivation of original holiness and justice, but human nature has not been totally corrupted: it is wounded in the natural powers proper to it, subject to ignorance, suffering and the dominion of death, and inclined to sin - an inclination to evil that is called "concupiscence." (CCC 405)

Original sin, therefore, is not something we do; it's something we suffer. Or, even more accurately, it's something we lack. We lack the grace necessary for becoming the people God made us to be. We lack the grace necessary for knowing the truth and choosing the good readily, easily, and happily.

Because we lack that grace and because of concupiscence (our inclination to do evil), we commit individual sins of our own. We make bad choices of our own, and each sin we commit compounds the consequences of original sin. Each sin adds evil and confusion to the world. Each sin further weakens and destroys the fundamental relationships of humans to each other, to nature, and to God. Each sin makes it harder for us to know the truth and choose the good, clouding our vision and weakening our wills all the more.

In a very real sense, what happened in the Fall happens every day in each of our lives. Every day, we pridefully take God's place in determining what is good and evil for ourselves, and every day we suffer the pains of that choice. This is the reason why it's difficult to accept God's offer of friendship. This is why we seek fulfillment by chasing after things that can never, ultimately, fulfill us. This is why so many people go through life with a God-shaped hole in their heart, refusing to do and love the very things that would help fill that hole.

If you ever find yourself struggling to know, love, and choose the good, know that you are not alone. This is the human experience. The unity of human nature and the human community has ensured that what happened in the Fall fundamentally scarred all of us. "For as by one man's disobedience many [that is, all men] were made sinners," explained St. Paul (Rom 5:19). Elsewhere, he noted, "sin came into the world through one man and death through sin, and so death spread to all men because all men sinned . . ." (Rom 5:12).

The Promise of Redemption

|| ASSIGNED READING
|| Genesis 3:14–15

Sin is the bad news. But there is good news, too. The same unity that made the action of one person detrimental to all also created the possibility of salvation for all. By one person's choice sin and death entered into the world. So, also by one person's choice, salvation entered the world. St. Paul continues, "Then as one man's trespass led to condemnation for all men, so one man's act of righteousness leads to acquittal and life for all men" (Rom 5:18).

This salvation was announced at the same moment that humanity's punishment for sin was announced. Even though Adam and Eve rejected

God, God did not reject them. Instead, he immediately promised a savior, the Messiah: "I will put enmity between you and the woman, and between your seed and her seed; he shall bruise your head, and you shall bruise his heel" (Gen 3:15).

This promise, often called the protoevangelium, which means "the first gospel," was made more concrete by the prophets of Israel and was ultimately fulfilled in Jesus Christ, who is this promised savior and the very means of our redemption. He is the Son of God, the Second Person of the Holy Trinity, the Word through which Creation came to be. For love of us, though, he became man, taking on flesh in the Incarnation.

The Catechism of the Catholic Church tells us that the Son of God became the Son of Man for four primary reasons (457–460).

First, he came to save us; he came to give us back the life that sin took from us and open up the possibility of eternal happiness once more by reconciling us to God: "he was revealed to take away sins," [1] wrote the Apostle John (1 John 3:5).

Second, Jesus came to show us the love of God, to give God's love flesh and make it visible and concrete: "For God so loved the world that he gave his only-begotten Son, that whoever believes in him should not perish but have eternal life" (John 3:16).

Third, Jesus came to be our model for holiness. "Take my yoke upon you, and learn from me . . ." he urged (Matt 11:29). "Listen to him!" echoed the Father (Luke 9:35).

Fourth, he came to make us partakers of the divine nature—to divinize us, to make us more like God in the way we were always meant to be more like God—through doing the things that truly fulfill our nature, listening to God, and not trying to be our own gods. "For this is why the Word became man, and the Son of God became the Son of man: so that man, by entering into communion with the Word and thus receiving divine sonship, might become a son of God." St. Irenaeus boldly asserted.[2]

As Jesus summed it up to his followers, "I am the way, and the truth, and the life" (John 14:6). That is to say, Jesus is the way back to friend-

---

[1] NABRE
[2] St. Irenaeus, *Adv. haeres.* 3, 19, 1: PG 7/1, 939, quoted in CCC 460.

ship with God. Jesus is the way back to the life for which we were made (Acts 4:12). Jesus is the way to true fulfillment, true happiness, true joy. Through a relationship with Jesus, we can begin reclaiming what was lost in Eden by our first parents. As our savior, our model, our guide, and our God, Jesus offers us everything we need to fill the hole in our heart, including the Church.

SELECTED READING
John Paul II, Encyclical Letter on the Value and Inviolability of Human Life *Evangelium Vitae* (March 25, 1995), nos. 34–36

Life is always a good. This is an instinctive perception and a fact of experience, and man is called to grasp the profound reason why this is so.

Why is life a good? This question is found everywhere in the Bible, and from the very first pages it receives a powerful and amazing answer. The life which God gives man is quite different from the life of all other living creatures, inasmuch as man, although formed from the dust of the earth (cf. Gen 2:7, 3:19; Job 34:15; Ps 103:14; 104:29), is a manifestation of God in the world, a sign of his presence, a trace of his glory (cf. Gen 1:26–27; Ps 8:6). This is what Saint Irenaeus of Lyons wanted to emphasize in his celebrated definition: "Man, living man, is the glory of God." Man has been given a sublime dignity, based on the intimate bond which unites him to his Creator: in man there shines forth a reflection of God himself.

The Book of Genesis affirms this when, in the first account of creation, it places man at the summit of God's creative activity, as its crown, at the culmination of a process which leads from indistinct chaos to the most perfect of creatures. Everything in creation is ordered to man and everything is made subject to him: "Fill the earth and subdue it; and have dominion over . . . every living thing" (1:28); this is God's command to the man and the woman. A similar message is found also in the other account of creation: "The Lord

God took the man and put him in the garden of Eden to till it and keep it" (Gen 2:15). We see here a clear affirmation of the primacy of man over things; these are made subject to him and entrusted to his responsible care, whereas for no reason can he be made subject to other men and almost reduced to the level of a thing.

In the biblical narrative, the difference between man and other creatures is shown above all by the fact that only the creation of man is presented as the result of a special decision on the part of God, a deliberation to establish a particular and specific bond with the Creator: "Let us make man in our image, after our likeness" (Gen 1:26). The life which God offers to man is a gift by which God shares something of himself with his creature.

Israel would ponder at length the meaning of this particular bond between man and God. The Book of Sirach too recognizes that God, in creating human beings, "endowed them with strength like his own, and made them in his own image" (17:3). The biblical author sees as part of this image not only man's dominion over the world but also those spiritual faculties which are distinctively human, such as reason, discernment between good and evil, and free will: "He filled them with knowledge and understanding, and showed them good and evil" (Sir 17:7). The ability to attain truth and freedom are human prerogatives inasmuch as man is created in the image of his Creator, God who is true and just (cf. Dt 32:4). Man alone, among all visible creatures, is "capable of knowing and loving his Creator." The life which God bestows upon man is much more than mere existence in time. It is a drive towards fullness of life; it is the seed of an existence which transcends the very limits of time: 'For God created man for incorruption, and made him in the image of his own eternity" (Wis 2:23).

The [second] account of creation expresses the same conviction. This ancient narrative speaks of a divine breath which is breathed into man so that he may come to life: "The Lord God formed man of dust from the ground, and breathed into his nostrils the breath of life; and man became a living being" (Gen 2:7).

The divine origin of this spirit of life explains the perennial dissatisfaction which man feels throughout his days on earth. Because he is made by God and bears within himself an indelible imprint of God, man is naturally drawn to God. When he heeds the deepest yearnings of the heart, every man must make his own the words of truth expressed by Saint Augustine: "You have made us for yourself, O Lord, and our hearts are restless until they rest in you."

How very significant is the dissatisfaction which marks man's life in Eden as long as his sole point of reference is the world of plants and animals (cf. Gen 2:20). Only the appearance of the woman, a being who is flesh of his flesh and bone of his bones (cf. Gen 2:23), and in whom the spirit of God the Creator is also alive, can satisfy the need for interpersonal dialogue, so vital for human existence. In the other, whether man or woman, there is a reflection of God himself, the definitive goal and fulfilment of every person.

"What is man that you are mindful of him, and the son of man that you care for him?" the Psalmist wonders (Ps 8:4). Compared to the immensity of the universe, man is very small, and yet this very contrast reveals his greatness: "You have made him little less than a god, and crown him with glory and honour" (Ps 8:5). The glory of God shines on the face of man. In man the Creator finds his rest, as Saint Ambrose comments with a sense of awe: "The sixth day is finished and the creation of the world ends with the formation of that masterpiece which is man, who exercises dominion over all living creatures and is as it were the crown of the universe and the supreme beauty of every created being. Truly we should maintain a reverential silence, since the Lord rested from every work he had undertaken in the world. He rested then in the depths of man, he rested in man's mind and in his thought; after all, he had created man endowed with reason, capable of imitating him, of emulating his virtue, of hungering for heavenly graces. In these his gifts God reposes, who has said: 'Upon whom shall I rest, if not upon the one who is humble, contrite in spirit and trembles at my word?' (Is 66:1–2). I thank the Lord our God who has created so wonderful a work in which to take his rest."

Unfortunately, God's marvelous plan was marred by the appearance of sin in history. Through sin, man rebels against his Creator and ends up by worshipping creatures: "They exchanged the truth about God for a lie and worshipped and served the creature rather than the Creator" (Rom 1:25). As a result man not only deforms the image of God in his own person, but is tempted to offences against it in others as well, replacing relationships of communion by attitudes of distrust, indifference, hostility and even murderous hatred. When God is not acknowledged as God, the profound meaning of man is betrayed and communion between people is compromised.

In the life of man, God's image shines forth anew and is again revealed in all its fullness at the coming of the Son of God in human flesh. "Christ is the image of the invisible God" (Col 1:15), he "reflects the glory of God and bears the very stamp of his nature" (Heb 1:3). He is the perfect image of the Father.

The plan of life given to the first Adam finds at last its fulfilment in Christ. Whereas the disobedience of Adam had ruined and marred God's plan for human life and introduced death into the world, the redemptive obedience of Christ is the source of grace poured out upon the human race, opening wide to everyone the gates of the kingdom of life (cf. Rom 5:12–21). As the Apostle Paul states: "The first man Adam became a living being; the last Adam became a life-giving spirit" (1 Cor 15:45).

All who commit themselves to following Christ are given the fullness of life: the divine image is restored, renewed and brought to perfection in them. God's plan for human beings is this, that they should "be conformed to the image of his Son" (Rom 8:29). Only thus, in the splendour of this image, can man be freed from the slavery of idolatry, rebuild lost fellowship and rediscover his true identity.

QUESTIONS FOR REVIEW

1. What is Original Innocence?
2. When Adam and Eve listened to the Serpent, who or what were they really rejecting?

3. What were four consequences of Adam and Eve's fall from grace?
4. What consequences of Adam and Eve's sin have we inherited from them? Explain.
5. What is the protoevangelium? Who fulfills it?

QUESTIONS FOR DISCUSSION

1. What are some of the conflicts you see in the world around you? Why do you think these conflicts exist? What desire is at the heart of the conflict?
2. Have you ever known what the right thing to do was and, in some way, wanted to do it, but still did the wrong thing? Describe. How does this correspond to the subjects discussed in Part I of this book?
3. Does the Church's teaching on original sin and concupiscence help you make sense of the world in which we live? Why or why not?

Chapter 3

Our Response to God's Plan

God made us. He gave us the power to know, the desire to love, and the freedom to choose. He now asks us to use what he's given us to know him, love him, and choose him. Moreover, when humanity broke faith with him, he became one of us, taking on flesh in the Incarnation, dying on the Cross, and rising again, so that we can say yes to what he asks of us—we can be reconciled to him, experience his love, understand how to live, and become more like him.

God has given us one gift after another. And despite all the ways in which we fail to love him and others as we should, he still calls us to eternal happiness with him. How can we respond to this call? How can we respond to all the gifts he gives?

The short answer is love. Love fulfills the commandments perfectly. Love is the primary means by which we are united with God. Love is the proper response to God's call to beatitude. But what does love look like in action? What shape should loving God and loving others take in the midst of our daily lives?

The answer to this question begins with Jesus Christ. Remember, the Son of God became man not just to save us from our sin, but also to show us how to attain happiness—or "beatitude"—in this life and the next.

The English word "beatitude" is a translation of the Greek word *makarios*. *Makarios* could also be translated as happy, blessed, or flourishing. To attain this joy, this beatitude, we must follow the example of Jesus. We must allow Jesus to live through us. We must be conformed to

Jesus. And we must receive his grace.

We do this first through the Sacrament of Baptism. In Baptism we receive the gift of sanctifying grace—God's own life—that Adam and Eve lost in the garden (CCC 1214). With that life in us, we are conformed to Christ. We become members of Christ's Body, the Church, and are adopted as sons and daughters of God, on the pattern of Christ (Eph 1:5).

Because of this, the focus of the moral life is living in accord with the gift we have been given. It's lived in accord with our new status as a son or daughter of God, a status received through the graces of Baptism. "Therefore, if any one is in Christ, he is a new creation; the old has passed away, behold, the new has come" (2 Cor 5:17).

But while this new life in Christ begins in Baptism, it doesn't end in Baptism. Rather, Baptism marks just the first step in our journey to holiness.

Our Vocation to Holiness

|| ASSIGNED READING
|| Romans 6

Holiness is something we often think of in connection with the Church's great saints. It can seem remote, unattainable, the sort of thing reserved for just a few special followers of Jesus. But that's not how God sees it. God's call to beatitude is really a call to holiness, and that call is for every single Christian. The Church often describes this as the "universal vocation."

Vocation comes from the Latin word, *vocatio*, which means "a calling." The universal vocation to holiness simply means that all are called to holiness; all are called to be set apart and dedicated to God. God doesn't want just a few of his followers to be saints; he wants all of us to be saints. He wants all of us to grow in love and live as mature Christian disciples in this world, so that we can live forever with him in the next. *Lumen Gentium* 39 makes this plain, saying: "in the Church, everyone whether belonging to the hierarchy, or being cared for by it, is called to holiness."[1]

This life of discipleship, at its most basic, is a life of witness. It's a life of not only knowing Jesus and loving Jesus, but also sharing that love and knowledge with the world through our words and actions. Jesus asks each of us to "love one another; even as I have loved you . . ." (John 13:34).

This is no easy task. Jesus suffered and died for love of us. He was mocked, beaten, tortured, and crucified for love of us. His love for us—a love demonstrated in concrete actions—demanded everything of him. And the love he asks us to give in return requires nothing less. It doesn't necessarily require that we be beaten and crucified. But it does requires selflessness, sacrifice, heroic generosity, and a willingness to be made a fool for Christ. To answer God's call to sainthood, to discipleship, to being witnesses of love is the most courageous thing we will ever do. The Catechism reminds us:

> The way of perfection passes by way of the Cross. There is no holiness without renunciation and spiritual battle [Cf. 2 Tim 4]. Spiritual progress entails the ascesis and mortification that gradually lead to living in the peace and joy of the Beatitudes: He who climbs never stops going from beginning to beginning, through beginnings that have no end. He never stops desiring what he already knows [St. Gregory of Nyssa, *Hom. In Cant.* 8: PG 44, 941C]. (CCC 2015)

It's also the most rewarding thing we will ever do. To become a saint is to become who we were made to be. And to walk the path to sainthood is to walk the path God made us to walk. It's to do the things we were made to do and, in that, find the fulfillment we desire. Every step of our journey to holiness is a step that helps us to grow in happiness.

What steps then, must we take? What does the life of discipleship require of us? What does love demand of us? That's where the Church's teachings on the moral life come in. Through those teachings, we can

---

[1] Second Vatican Council, Dogmatic Constitution on the Church *Lumen Gentium* (November 21, 1964), §39.

start to discern what Jesus asks of us on a practical level. Moral theology is, ultimately, a guide to happiness. It's the map that shows us to the way to heaven. And to that map we now turn.

SELECTED READING
Benedict XVI, Encyclical Letter on Christian Hope *Spe Salvi* (November 30, 2007), nos. 24–27

Let us ask once again: what may we hope? And what may we not hope? First of all, we must acknowledge that incremental progress is possible only in the material sphere. Here, amid our growing knowledge of the structure of matter and in the light of ever more advanced inventions, we clearly see continuous progress towards an ever greater mastery of nature. Yet in the field of ethical awareness and moral decision-making, there is no similar possibility of accumulation for the simple reason that man's freedom is always new and he must always make his decisions anew. These decisions can never simply be made for us in advance by others—if that were the case, we would no longer be free. Freedom presupposes that in fundamental decisions, every person and every generation is a new beginning. Naturally, new generations can build on the knowledge and experience of those who went before, and they can draw upon the moral treasury of the whole of humanity. But they can also reject it, because it can never be self-evident in the same way as material inventions. The moral treasury of humanity is not readily at hand like tools that we use; it is present as an appeal to freedom and a possibility for it. This, however, means that:

a. The right state of human affairs, the moral well-being of the world can never be guaranteed simply through structures alone, however good they are. Such structures are not only important, but necessary; yet they cannot and must not marginalize human freedom. Even the best structures function only when the community is animated by convictions capable of motivating people to assent freely to the social order. Freedom requires conviction; conviction does not exist on its own, but *must always be gained anew by the community.*

b. Since man always remains free and since his freedom is always fragile, the kingdom of good will never be definitively established in this world. Anyone who promises the better world that is guaranteed to last for ever is making a false promise; he is overlooking human freedom. Freedom must constantly be won over for the cause of good. Free assent to the good never exists simply by itself. If there were structures which could irrevocably guarantee a determined—good—state of the world, man's freedom would be denied, and hence they would not be good structures at all.

What this means is that every generation has the task of engaging anew in the arduous search for the right way to order human affairs; this task is never simply completed. Yet every generation must also make its own contribution to establishing convincing structures of freedom and of good, which can help the following generation as a guideline for the proper use of human freedom; hence, always within human limits, they provide a certain guarantee also for the future. In other words: good structures help, but of themselves they are not enough. Man can never be redeemed simply from outside. Francis Bacon and those who followed in the intellectual current of modernity that he inspired were wrong to believe that man would be redeemed through science. Such an expectation asks too much of science; this kind of hope is deceptive. Science can contribute greatly to making the world and mankind more human. Yet it can also destroy mankind and the world unless it is steered by forces that lie outside it. On the other hand, we must also acknowledge that modern Christianity, faced with the successes of science in progressively structuring the world, has to a large extent restricted its attention to the individual and his salvation. In so doing it has limited the horizon of its hope and has failed to recognize sufficiently the greatness of its task—even if it has continued to achieve great things in the formation of man and in care for the weak and the suffering.

It is not science that redeems man: man is redeemed by love. This applies even in terms of this present world. When someone has the experience of a great love in his life, this is a moment of "redemption" which gives a new meaning to his life. But soon he will also realize that the love bestowed upon him cannot by itself resolve the question of his life. It is a love that remains fragile. It can be destroyed by death. The human being needs unconditional love. He needs the certainty which makes him say: "neither death, nor life, nor angels, nor principalities, nor things present, nor things to come, nor powers, nor height, nor depth, nor anything else in all creation, will be able to separate us from the love of God in Christ Jesus our Lord" (Rom 8:38–39). If this absolute love exists, with its absolute certainty, then—only then—is man "redeemed," whatever should happen to him in his particular circumstances. This is what it means to say: Jesus Christ has "redeemed" us. Through him we have become certain of God, a God who is not a remote "first cause" of the world, because his only-begotten Son has become man and of him everyone can say: "I live by faith in the Son of God, who loved me and gave himself for me" (Gal 2:20).

In this sense it is true that anyone who does not know God, even though he may entertain all kinds of hopes, is ultimately without hope, without the great hope that sustains the whole of life (cf. Eph 2:12). Man's great, true hope which holds firm in spite of all disappointments can only be God—God who has loved us and who continues to love us "to the end," until all "is accomplished" (cf. Jn 13:1 and 19:30). Whoever is moved by love begins to perceive what "life" really is. He begins to perceive the meaning of the word of hope that we encountered in the Baptismal Rite: from faith I await "eternal life"—the true life which, whole and unthreatened, in all its fullness, is simply life. Jesus, who said that he had come so that we might have life and have it in its fullness, in abundance (cf. Jn 10:10), has also explained to us what "life" means: "this is eternal life, that they know you the only true God, and Jesus Christ *whom you have sent*" (Jn 17:3). Life in its true sense is not something we have exclusively in or from ourselves: it is a relationship. And life in its totality is a relationship with him who is the source of life. If we are in relation with him who does not die, who is Life itself and Love itself, then we are in life. Then we "live."

QUESTIONS FOR REVIEW

1. How are we called to respond to all the gifts God has given us?
2. What does the word "beatitude" mean, and how do we attain it?
3. What makes us adopted sons and daughters of God?
4. What is a vocation to holiness?
5. Whom does God call to sainthood?

QUESTIONS FOR DISCUSSION

1. Who are the people who have given you the most and cared for you the most? How do you respond to them for that love? What do you do for them in return?
2. What are some of the good gifts God has given you? Be specific. How do you show your gratitude? Do you show—or even feel—gratitude? Why or why not?
3. Is it hard to think of yourself becoming holy or a saint? Why or why not?

Chapter 4

Human Happiness and the Law

Every human person wants to be happy. This is how God made us. To want to be happy is simply to want what God wants for us. At the same time, it's important to recognize that wanting to be happy is different from knowing what happiness is and seeking it in the right way.

More than two thousand years ago, before Jesus Christ came to earth, the great Greek philosophers Aristotle and Plato wrestled with the meaning of happiness. In fact, they believed the most important question a person could ask is, "What is happiness?" As they reasoned, happiness is the goal of the whole moral life; it's also the goal of every particular action we take. Accordingly, if we don't know what happiness is, we can't know if particular actions will further our happiness (making those actions good) or inhibit our happiness (making those actions bad).

Essentially, Aristotle and Plato understood that we need to know and understand the goal before reflecting on the means. Catholic moral theology agrees with them. Happiness is the whole goal of the moral life, so if we don't understand happiness, we can't intentionally make good moral choices. We can't discern the best means without knowing the end we're seeking.

So, what is happiness? The answer begins with that God-shaped hole in our heart that we talked about in Chapter 1. Each of us longs for infinite joy, infinite love, infinite satisfaction. Having what we long for is happiness. But nothing finite can fill an infinite hole. The only thing that can fill it—the only thing that can fulfill our longing for infinite joy, love, and satisfaction—is a relationship with the infinite God. Only when we know him, love him, and are in a relationship with him can we truly be happy. Quoting St. Augustine, the Catechism tells us:

> Man is made to live in communion with God in whom he finds happiness: When I am completely united to you, there will be no more sorrow or trials; entirely full of you, my life will be complete (St Augustine, *Conf.* 10, 28, 39: PL 32, 795). (CCC 45)

Happiness, therefore, is eternally contemplating and loving the Triune God through Jesus Christ. Understanding how to attain this goal is the whole purpose of Catholic moral theology. We need to know what actions will bring us closer to God—what actions enable us to receive his love and give him love in return. We also need to know what actions will harm our relationship with God. The law helps give us this knowledge.

The Nature of the Law

Oftentimes, when we think of law, we think of rules and regulations imposed on people by the governing authorities. Sometimes these rules seem wise. Sometimes they seem arbitrary. Sometimes they serve our interests. Sometimes they clearly serve the interests of those in power. Because unwise and self-serving laws exist, it's easy to think of law in a negative sense, as something that limits our freedom and prevents us from doing or having what we want. But that is not how God's laws work. God's laws actually make us more free and enable us to do and have what we want. In order to understand how this works, we first need to distinguish between different types of laws.

Laws, as Thomas Aquinas teaches, are "dictates of reason promulgated by the proper authority for the common good."[1] These laws exist to shape human behavior. True laws exist to promote good actions and dissuade bad actions. Another way to express this idea is that true laws

---

[1] Aquinas, ST I-II, q. 90, a. 4.

THE NATURE OF THE LAW

exist to promote acts of virtue and prohibit acts of vice. In short, law exists to promote true human freedom. As Pope St. John Paul II explains in *Veritatis Splendor*, "God's law does not reduce, much less do away with human freedom; rather, it protects and promotes that freedom."[2]

A real law, a law that can promote virtue and prohibit vice, has all four of the aspects outlined by St. Thomas. If a law lacks any of these aspects—if it is not reasonable, if it is not properly promulgated, if it is not made by the proper authority, or if it is not for the common good—then it is not a true law. Now, this doesn't mean that if a law isn't a true law, that we should automatically disobey it. There might be good reasons, at least in the short run, for obeying an unjust law. But unjust laws do create both the conditions and the justification for disobedience (CCC 2242).

Types of Laws

St. Thomas Aquinas gave us our definition of law above. He also helps us understand the differences between laws. This is important, because all laws are not the same. Catholic theology actually recognizes four different types of law: eternal law, divine law, natural law, and civil law (CCC 1952).

All these types of laws get the name "law" from their participation in the eternal law, which is, as St. Thomas Aquinas tells us, the very foundation and fundamental law of all things (CCC 1951).[3] Essentially, eternal law is God's plan of the world. It's the means by which God governs and orders all of creation. In a sense, it's like an architect's rendering of a building or a sculptor's preliminary sketch of a statue. From all eternity, God had an idea of the world—of what it would look like and how it would operate. That idea is eternal law. It's God's wisdom, his divine providence, directing all things to their proper fulfillment and perfection.

Natural law is how human beings participate in eternal law (CCC 1955). It's how *we* fit into God's design of the universe. Natural law doesn't apply to dogs or cats, the movement of oceans, or the movement

---

[2] John Paul II, Encyclical Letter Regarding Certain Fundamental Questions of the Church's Moral Teaching *Veritatis Splendor* (August 6, 1993), §35.

[3] Aquinas, ST I-II, q. 91, a. 1.

of stars. Those things are governed by the laws of nature, which is an entirely different thing from natural law. Both types of law are ordained by God, but the laws of nature order the natural world, while natural law orders humanity's moral world. Natural law helps us know, as human beings, which actions will make us happy and which actions will make us unhappy. In other words, natural law helps us live in accord with God's plan for *our* nature, our human nature. It helps us to do good and avoid evil (which is considered the first principle of the natural law).

Likewise, because the natural law is fitted to our nature, it provides the foundation for all basic human rights (CCC 1956). The right to life, the right to marriage and procreation, the right to food and water—all of these are rooted in the natural law. They are rights because they are essential to human flourishing; they are essential to men and women living the lives God made us to live. Likewise, because they are rooted in our human nature, these rights are common to all people. It doesn't matter where you live, the color of your skin, or the state of your health; if you are human, you possess certain basic, fundamental rights.

With rights, however, come duties. Just as the natural law says we should have certain rights as human beings, it also says we have certain responsibilities. The first precept (command) of the natural law is the same as the first principle of natural law: do good and avoid evil. So, we have a duty to do those things that perfect human nature and avoid those things that corrupt human nature.

Importantly, while each type of law is distinct, the laws of God are meant to guide us to happiness. The law is God's "fatherly instruction, God's pedagogy" (CCC 1950). Accordingly, because God, like any good teacher (or good parent) never contradicts himself, all his laws are related and connected to one another (CCC 1952).

In theory, civil laws—the laws of our countries, states, and cities—should also be related to the other forms of law. Although civil laws (unlike the natural law) can be different in different times and places, they should still share the same goal as God's laws—human happiness—and they all should be rooted in the natural law. That is to say, they should find their basis in what will most aid human flourishing. This isn't always the case, though.

Consider, for example, the United States' abortion laws. In the US, it is legal to abort a child at almost any stage of its development. That is an American civil law. But, this particular civil law denies the unborn human person their most fundamental right according to the natural law: the right to life. In this case, the civil law is contrary to the natural law, which makes the civil law of abortion an unjust law. This is how we judge a civil law: we measure it against the natural law. Just civil laws are rooted in the natural law. Unjust civil laws violate the natural law.

Simple reason should allow us to see that. And yet, for many people, it doesn't. Why? The answer is bound up with original sin.

Because each of us possesses a human nature, each of us also possesses reason, which helps us discern the natural law. In theory, we don't need Revelation to help us know that we need to do good and avoid evil—that we need to pay our debts, care for our families, not harm the innocent, and do a host of other activities that fall within the purview of natural law. But original sin and the concupiscence that results from it cloud our reason and corrupt our desires, so what should be clear to us often isn't and what we should desire we often don't.

For these reasons, God has revealed his plan for our perfection through the divine law (CCC 1955). The divine law not only helps us to know the natural law more precisely, but also perfects the natural law, calling us to more than just natural perfection and natural happiness (a happiness proportionate with human nature), but also to supernatural perfection and supernatural happiness (a perfection and happiness that far exceeds our nature and is a participation in God's own perfection and happiness).

Revelation and the Law

Divine law comes to us in two forms: the Old Law and the New Law. Although the qualifiers "old" and "new," can make us think that only one law—the new one—is relevant to us, that's not the case. Old, in this case, doesn't mean "outdated"; it means "preparatory."

The Old Law prepared God's people for the Gospel. It did that by revealing to the Israelites what they should have known simply by virtue of their reason, but often didn't. This revelation is summed up in the Ten Commandments (CCC 1962–1963). The Ten Commandments make explicit the implicit natural law discernable by reason. What concupiscence confuses, the Ten Commandments clarify. They are God's revelation in time of what we can know naturally but often don't know (or only know in part). God gives us this revelation so that we can know the demands of the natural law with certainty, quickly, and without error

As good as the Old Law was (and is), though, by itself it remains imperfect. It really does reveal God's will for human activity—love of God and neighbor—but it doesn't enable us to do God's will. It tells us what our darkened intellects can no longer see, but it doesn't give our weak wills the help they need to do what the law tells us to do. Hence, as St. Paul says, the law is experienced as a bondage (Rom 7). This is why we need the New Law.

The New Law isn't preparation for the Gospel. It is the Gospel (CCC 1965). In the New Law, Jesus frees us from the bondage experienced under the Old Law, not by doing away with the Ten Commandments, but by bringing them to completion and perfection.

What Jesus does is take the external law, the law experienced as bondage, and writes it anew on our hearts (Jer 31:33). This not only underlines the continuing importance of the Ten Commandments, but also enables those commandments to liberate us—to make us truly free—through God's grace. The very heart of the New Law is not the external command to do this or avoid that, but rather the interior dwelling of the Holy Spirit. With the life of God dwelling in us, it becomes not only easier to do God's will, but increasingly joyful and fulfilling. The more God lives in us, the more continuously his grace abides in us, the more natural and simple it becomes to do the good.

The New Law is, ultimately, a law of love and freedom. The Catechism explains:

> The New Law is called a *law of love* because it makes us act out of the love infused by the Holy Spirit, rather than from fear; a *law of grace*, because it confers the strength of grace to act, by means of faith and the sacraments; a *law of freedom*, because it sets us

free from the ritual and juridical observances of the Old Law, inclines us to act spontaneously by the prompting of charity and, finally, lets us pass from the condition of a servant who "does not know what his master is doing" to that of a friend of Christ—"For all that I have heard from my Father I have made known to you"—or even to the status of son and heir [*Jn* 15:15; cf. *Jas* 2:12 ;1:25; *Gal* 4:1–7, 21–31; *Rom* 8:15]. (CCC 1972)

Here, it's important to note that the Church's understanding of the demands of both the Old and New Law has continued to grow and deepen through the centuries. Guided by the Holy Spirit, the Apostles and their successors in history—the Church's bishops—have continued to reflect upon the requirements of the both the New Law and the Old Law and apply them anew to each generation. The teachings of the law can never change, but as new problems and challenges emerge in time—such as communism, internet pornography, or climate change—the Church's magisterium has the wisdom and authority necessary to discern how the law applies to these challenges and help us learn how to navigate them.

SELECTED READING
John Paul II, Encyclical Letter *Veritatis Splendor* (August 6, 1993), nos. 42–44

Patterned on God's freedom, man's freedom is not negated by his obedience to the divine law; indeed, only through this obedience does it abide in the truth and conform to human dignity. This is clearly stated by the Council: "Human dignity requires man to act through conscious and free choice, as motivated and prompted personally from within, and not through blind internal impulse or merely external pressure. Man achieves such dignity when he frees himself from all subservience to his feelings, and in a free choice of the good, pursues his own end by effectively and assiduously marshalling the appropriate means."

In his journey towards God, the One who "alone is good," man must freely do good and avoid evil. But in order to accomplish this he must *be able to distinguish good from evil*. And this takes place above all *thanks to the light of natural reason*, the reflection in man of the splendor of God's countenance. Thus Saint Thomas, commenting on a verse of Psalm 4, writes: "After saying: Offer right sacrifices (Ps 4:5), as if some had then asked him what right works were, the Psalmist adds: *There are many who say: Who will make us see good?* And in reply to the question he says: *The light of your face, Lord, is signed upon us*, thereby implying that the light of natural reason whereby we discern good from evil, which is the function of the natural law, is nothing else but an imprint on us of the divine light." It also becomes clear why this law is called the natural law: it receives this name not because it refers to the nature of irrational beings but because the reason which promulgates it is proper to human nature.

The Second Vatican Council points out that the "supreme rule of life is the divine law itself, the eternal, objective and universal law by which God out of his wisdom and love arranges, directs and governs the whole world and the paths of the human community. God has enabled man to share in this divine law, and hence man is able under the gentle guidance of God's providence increasingly to recognize the unchanging truth."

The Council refers back to the classic teaching on *God's eternal law*. Saint Augustine defines this as "the reason or the will of God, who commands us to respect the natural order and forbids us to disturb it." Saint Thomas identifies it with "the type of the divine wisdom as moving all things to their due end." And God's wisdom is providence, a love which cares. God himself loves and cares, in the most literal and basic sense, for all creation (cf. Wis 8:11 ;7:22). But God provides for man differently from the way in which he provides for beings which are not persons. He cares for man not "from without," through the laws of physical nature, but "from within," through reason, which, by its natural knowledge of God's eternal law, is consequently able to show man the right direction to take in his free actions. In this way God calls man to participate in his own providence, since he desires to guide the world—not only the world of nature but also the world of human persons—through man himself, through man's reasonable and responsible care. The *natural law* enters here as the human expression of God's eternal law. Saint Thomas writes: "Among all others, the rational creature is subject to divine providence in the most excellent way, insofar as it partakes of a share of providence, being provident both for itself and for others. Thus it has a share of the Eternal Reason, whereby it has a natural inclination to its proper act and end. This participation of the eternal law in the rational creature is called natural law."

The Church has often made reference to the Thomistic doctrine of natural law, including it in her own teaching on morality. Thus my Venerable Predecessor Leo XIII emphasized *the essential subordination of reason and human law to the Wisdom of God and to his law*. After stating that "the natural law is written and engraved in the heart of each and every man, since it is none other than human reason itself which commands us to do good and counsels us not to sin," Leo XIII appealed to the "higher reason" of the divine Lawgiver: "But this prescription of human reason could not have the force of law unless it were the voice and the interpreter of some higher reason to which our spirit and our freedom must be subject." Indeed, the force of law consists in its authority to impose duties, to confer rights and to sanction certain behavior: "Now all of this, clearly, could not exist in man if, as his own supreme legislator, he gave himself the rule of his own actions." And he concluded: "It follows that the natural law is *itself the eternal law*, implanted in beings endowed with reason, and inclining them *towards their right action and end*; it is none other than the eternal reason of the Creator and Ruler of the universe."

Man is able to recognize good and evil thanks to that discernment of good from evil which he himself carries out by his *reason, in particular by his reason enlightened by Divine Revelation and by faith*, through the law which God gave to the Chosen People, beginning with the commandments on Sinai. Israel was called to accept and to live out God's *law as a particular gift and sign of its election and of the divine Covenant*, and also as a pledge of God's blessing. Thus Moses could address the children of Israel and ask them: "What great nation is that that has a god so near to it as the Lord our God is to us, whenever we call upon him? And what great nation is there that has statutes and ordinances so righteous as all this law which I set before you this day?" (Dt 4:7–8). In the Psalms we encounter the sentiments of praise, gratitude and veneration which the Chosen People is called to show towards God's law, together with an exhortation to know it, ponder it and translate it into life. "Blessed is the man who walks not in the counsel of the wicked, nor stands in the way of sinners, nor sits in the seat of scoffers, but his delight is in the law of the Lord and on his law he meditates day and night" (Ps 1:1–2). "The law of the Lord is perfect, reviving the soul; the testimony of the Lord is sure, making wise the simple; the precepts of the Lord are right, rejoicing the heart; the commandment of the Lord is pure, enlightening the eyes" (Ps 1819:8–9).

QUESTIONS FOR REVIEW

1. What is true happiness?
2. For what purpose does the law exist?
3. What is eternal law?
4. What is natural law?
5. What is divine law? In what two form does it come to us?

QUESTIONS FOR DISCUSSION

1. When you hear the word "law," how do you react? Do you have good associations with the word or bad associations?
2. What are some examples of good laws—of laws that you are grateful for and recognize as good?
3. What would our world be like without laws? How has a law helped you or taught you something important?

PART II

GOD'S GUIDANCE IN THE OLD TESTAMENT:

THE TEN COMMANDMENTS

|| ASSIGNED READING
|| Exodus 12:1–20

The Ten Commandments form the moral heart of the Old Law. As an expression of the natural law, they continue to guide us today. They were first given to humanity, however, in the context of the Mosaic Covenant.

By now, you've probably heard the word "covenant" many times, and understand that covenants and contracts aren't the same thing. For example, unlike contracts, which form business arrangements between two parties, covenants form families. They form permanent bonds of kinship. Marriage is one form of a covenant. Adoption is another. Also, unlike contracts, which dictate the terms of an exchange of goods or services, covenants dictate the terms of an exchange of people. They dictate the terms by which people give themselves to one another.

In the Mosaic Covenant, God establishes the terms for his relationship with the nation of Israel. He swears to shepherd Israel, lead Israel, and raise Israel up to be a light to all the nations . . . if Israel, in turn, follows his commandments—that is, sticks to God's terms. God tells them:

> Now therefore, if you will obey my voice and keep my covenant,
> you shall be my own possession among all peoples; for all the
> earth is mine, and you shall be to me a kingdom of priests and
> a holy nation. These are the words which you shall speak to the
> children of Israel. (Exod 19:5–6)

The Ten Commandments were the central part of these covenantal
terms. They showed Israel how they should relate to both God (in the
First through Third Commandments) and their neighbor (in the Fourth
through Tenth Commandments). In showing Israel this, the Ten Commandments showed them how they could be truly free.

Because the Ten Commandments were revealed as part of the Mosaic
Covenant, one might think that they could be ignored today. But, unlike
the other legal and ceremonial precepts given by God to the Israelites in
the Mosaic Covenant, the Ten Commandments remain as much a part of
divine law as ever. Again, they are the Word of God about the dictates of
natural law. They were written on stone with God's own hand thousands
of years ago, and they reflect the deepest desires of the human heart from
the beginning of human history (Exod 31:18; Rom 2:14–15).

Chapter 1

THE FIRST THROUGH THIRD
COMMANDMENTS

The First Commandment: "I Am the Lord, Your God; You Shall Not Have Strange Gods Before Me."

The most important guidance God gives for the moral life is that he must come first. This makes perfect sense given that the ultimate goal always dictates how we pursue lesser goals. If you want to become a professional soccer player, then how you live your life—what you eat, how you exercise, the way you spend your free time—must be dictated by that goal. Likewise, if you want to go to Harvard for college, how you spend your time in high school—the classes you take, the hours you devote to studying, and the activities in which you participate—must be dictated by that goal.

It's the same—only more so—when it comes to achieving our ultimate end, our ultimate goal: holiness. If we want to be a saint, then we have to start putting God first now. He is our final end, so our relationship with him has to come before everything else.

It's easy to fool ourselves into thinking we already do this. That's because when most of us think of having other gods before God, we think of worshipping in a false religion or bowing down before an idol.

It's important not to do that: worshipping false gods and golden calves is definitely a violation of the First Commandment. But it's not the only way we can violate it.

Anytime we put anything before God—money, power, fame, pleasure, contentment, security, even our friends and family—we make an idol out of those things. If you skip Mass on Sunday so that you can get to your soccer game, soccer has become an idol. If you go along with what your friends want you to do, even though you know it's not what God wants you to do, you've made an idol out of your friends. If you care more about making money, looking a certain way, or getting good grades than you do about pleasing God, you are bowing down before idols. God tells us from the start: he is our Creator; he is our Final Goal; he, and he alone, can make us ultimately happy; so he has to come first. If we put anything else before him, it's not ultimately going to fulfill us. It's going to hurt us.

Besides making an idol out of people or things, we can break the First Commandment in a number of other ways.

For example, every time we willfully cultivate doubt—refusing to even wrestle with difficult questions of faith—or willfully refuse to accept some tenet of the faith, despite all the good reasons God has given us (known as motives of credibility and preambles of faith), we violate the First Commandment (CCC 2088). Heresy and schism (denying some truth of the faith or breaking away from the Catholic Church) are also sins against the First Commandment (CCC 2089). All these sins, at their heart, are a failure of faith. They're a failure of trust in God and his Church.

Presumption (thinking we don't need God and can save ourselves or can be saved without repentance and conversion) and despair (thinking our sins are so great that even God can't save us and redeem us) are likewise sins against the First Commandment (CCC 2091–2092). They're a failure to hope in God's mercy, and, in a sense, they signify us putting ourselves in God's place, making a god of either our own abilities or our own sins.

Sinning against God's love is yet another way we can fall short of the bar set for us by the First Commandment. We can do this through indifference (not giving sufficient thought to God's love); ingratitude (not giving sufficient thanks for God's love); lukewarmness (not responding quickly and eagerly to God's love and its promptings); acedia (refusing to be joyful—or even cultivating distaste—in the face of God's love); and hatred of God (denying God's love and resenting him). All these sins are failures of charity, a failure to respond to God's love with love (CCC 2092).

Other violations of the First Commandment include:

- Superstition: worshipping God in a false way or worshipping a false god. Examples of this are thinking black cats bring bad luck or knocking on wood so as not to jinx yourself (CCC 2111).
- Irreligion: behaving sacrilegiously or tempting God. Sacrilegious behavior could be doing something like selling holy objects, disfiguring a sacred painting, or receiving Holy Communion in a state of serious sin. Tempting God could be demanding God do something to prove himself to you or daring him to punish you for violating one of his commands (CCC 2118).
- Divination: attempting to control God and discover the future without God. Divinization comes in many forms: horoscopes, astrology, palm reading, omens and casting lots, clairvoyance, mediums, and even Magic 8 balls (CCC 2115–2116).
- Magic: attempting to tame and control occult powers. Used even for "good" purposes, magic is very sinful and extremely dangerous. The use of hexes, curses, alleged magical tinctures, and Ouija boards all fall into this category (CCC 2117).

The Second Commandment: You Shall Not Take the Name of the Lord, Your God, in Vain.

Long ago, while the Israelites still served as slaves in Egypt, God spoke to Moses from a burning bush. In that conversation, he revealed his name to Moses: I AM WHO I AM (Exod 3:14). That revelation was an act of trust and intimacy. It signified God making himself known to his Chosen People in a new and radical way. The Israelites recognized this and held God's name as sacred, refusing even to speak it out of fear of misusing it.

This is why the Jewish people became so angry with Jesus when he not only said the divine name, but also claimed it for himself: "Jesus said to them, 'Truly, truly, I say to you, before Abraham was, I am'" (John 8:58).

The coming of Jesus Christ and the familial intimacy established between God and his people in the New Covenant changed what it meant to respect the name of God. We're now free to speak God's name—to call him Father, Son, and Holy Spirit—because of our adoption in Jesus Christ. But the need for reverence of the divine name remains.

The Catechism states: "The name is the icon of the person. It demands respect as a sign of the dignity of the one who bears it" (CCC 2158). This holds true for every person, but it holds true in an even greater way for God, our Creator and Redeemer, whose infinite love and mercy deserve nothing but infinite respect. This means we "must keep [his name] in mind in silent, loving adoration" and not use it "except to bless, praise, and glorify It" (CCC 2143).

We fail to do this when we use God's name "in vain." This phrase can mean many things, starting with using God's name casually. To casually exclaim, "Oh my God!" "Jesus Christ!" "Holy Mother of God!" or "Jesus, Mary, and Joseph!" in conversation, surprise, frustration, boredom, or anger is taking God's name in vain. God and his saints are not phrases to be used for expressing emotions. An angry "God damn it" is also wrong. God is not a swear word, and damning things in his name isn't something anyone has a right to do (CCC 2145–2147).

We also take God's name in vain when we swear a false oath, or commit perjury (making a promise under oath when we have no intention of keeping it). If we take a solemn oath in God's name or if we "swear to God" that we are telling the truth or that we will do something, then we have a sacred obligation to tell the truth and keep our promise to the very best of our ability. This is because in swearing an oath to God or promising something in God's name, we have taken God as our witness. Which means if we don't honor that oath or keep our promise, we "make God out to be a liar [Cf. *1 Jn* 1:10]" (CCC 2147).

Blasphemy is yet another way we can fail to give God's name the respect it deserves. To blaspheme is to speak against God. It's to condemn him, curse him, reproach him, or defy him. It's also to use his name to cover up some wrong we have done or to do something wrong in his name. Importantly, the prohibition on blasphemy doesn't just apply to God's name. It also applies to his Church and his saints, as well as sacred things, such as the Eucharist or the Holy Cross (CCC 2148).

The Third Commandment: Remember to Keep Holy the Lord's Day

The Third Commandment, like the two before it, is focused on our relationship with God.

The tradition of a "Sabbath" rest was begun by God himself, who, after creating the world, rested on the seventh day (Gen 2:1–3). God, of course, didn't need to rest. He's God. He doesn't get tired. But we do, and by resting from work on the seventh day, God calls us to rest as well. Like any teacher, he models for us what he wants us to do: take a break from our work and the business of the world and attend instead to the business of eternity, which consists of resting in God and worshipping him.

This lesson is reinforced by the use of the number seven. In the Hebrew tradition, the number seven is the traditional number of completion or perfection. This is why God rests specifically on the seventh day: to help us see that worship perfects creation. All of creation finds its perfection—its ultimate fulfillment—in the worship of God.

Once the Israelites are liberated from captivity in Egypt, God gives them this command: to maintain a solemn rest and worship him on the seventh day. He asks them to do this as a way of memorializing their deliverance from slavery and their covenant with him. Every seven days, he instructs, they are to remember the great good he has done for them and the great gift he has given them in the Mosaic Covenant (Deut 5:15).

For nearly 1500 years, the Jewish people observed this Sabbath rest on Saturday—the seventh day. Not only did they worship God on the Sabbath, but they also refrained from every possible form of labor. When Jesus came, his insistence on doing good on the Sabbath—healing, teaching, and feeding people—scandalized many of the Jewish leaders. His response to them established for his followers a clear understanding of the Sabbath rest's purpose: "The sabbath was made for man, not man for the sabbath" (Mark 2:27). Or, as the Catechism explains:

> With compassion, Christ declares the Sabbath for doing good rather than harm, for saving life rather than killing [Cf. Mk 3:4]. The Sabbath is the day of the Lord of mercies and a day to honor God [Cf. Mt 12:5; Jn 7:23]. (CCC 2173)

The Jewish people continue to observe the Sabbath rest on Saturday, but after Jesus' Resurrection, Christians began celebrating our Sabbath rest on Sunday, the day the Lord rose from the dead, making all things new and marking the start of a new creation (2 Cor 5:17).

When we go to Mass on Sunday (or Saturday evening), we heed God's call to keep the Sabbath. Not only do we engage in the most fundamental aspect of the Sabbath rest—worship—but we also participate in the Eucharist, which is the sign and renewal of the New Covenant instituted by Jesus Christ (Luke 22:20).

The Eucharist makes Jesus substantially, really, and truly present. It erases the distance between the "then" of Christ's Incarnation and the "now" of our lives, making his saving death on the Cross present right in front of us. In this way, Sunday fulfills the spiritual truths of the Jewish Sabbath—as a day of rest, a day of worship, and a day of remembering the covenant, only the covenant we remember is the New Covenant in Jesus Christ.

Because of its nearness to the very heart of the Christian mystery, it is a serious sin to skip Mass on Sunday or a holy day of obligation. If we deliberately miss Mass, we reject God himself.

> The Sunday Eucharist is the foundation and confirmation of all Christian practice. For this reason the faithful are obliged to participate in the Eucharist on days of obligation, unless excused for a serious reason (for example, illness, the care of infants) or dispensed by their own pastor [Cf. CIC, can. 1245]. Those who deliberately fail in this obligation commit a grave sin. (CCC 2181)

As the Catechism notes above, there are good reasons for someone to miss Mass. If you're seriously ill, wounded, or contagious with a communicable virus (such as the stomach flu), you're not deliberately missing Mass. Likewise, if you're caring for someone who is seriously ill or injured and who needs constant attention, and there is no one available to relieve you, you're also not deliberately missing Mass. The same goes for not having transportation or any possible means of getting to Mass. Those are all valid reasons to not get to Church. Others exist as well. What counts as a serious reason is ultimately a matter of judgment. A good rule of thumb is that if it is a physical impossibility (you physically cannot go or it is very difficult) or a moral impossibility (you have to sin to make it to Mass), you are excused from Mass.

In addition to attending Mass on Sunday, observing the Sabbath rest also includes imitating God, who rested on the seventh day. This requires us to "refrain from engaging in work or activities that hinder the worship owed to God, the joy proper to the Lord's Day, the performance of the works of mercy, and the appropriate relaxation of mind and body [Cf. CIC, can. 120]" (CCC 2185).

Similarly, we must refrain from any unnecessary activities that preclude others' rest on Sunday. Some people, of course, have to work on Sunday—for example, doctors, nurses, policemen, and firefighters, who are all serving the common good. In other less essential cases, such as shopping, the Church asks us to not make unnecessary demands on others that would prevent them from honoring the Sabbath.

Rather than doing things that require others to work, the Church asks us to spend some of our Sunday doing works of mercy, preforming special acts of kindness or hospitality for those most in need: the physically and spiritually poor, the elderly, the lonely, prisoners, etc. (see Matt 25:31–46 and CCC 2447).

SELECTED READING
Benedict XVI, Post-Synodal Apostolic Exhortation on the
Eucharist as the Source and Summit of the Church's Life
and Mission *Sacramentum Caritatis* (February 22, 2007),
nos. 71–74

Christianity's new worship includes and transfigures every aspect of
life: "Whether you eat or drink, or whatever you do, do all to the
glory of God" (1 Cor 10:31). Christians, in all their actions, are
called to offer true worship to God. Here the intrinsically eucharistic
nature of Christian life begins to take shape. The Eucharist, since
it embraces the concrete, everyday existence of the believer, makes
possible, day by day, the progressive transfiguration of all those called
by grace to reflect the image of the Son of God (cf. Rom 8:29ff.).
There is nothing authentically human—our thoughts and affections,
our words and deeds—that does not find in the sacrament of the
Eucharist the form it needs to be lived to the full. Here we can see
the full human import of the radical newness brought by Christ in
the Eucharist: the worship of God in our lives cannot be relegated
to something private and individual, but tends by its nature to permeate every aspect of our existence. Worship pleasing to God thus
becomes a new way of living our whole life, each particular moment
of which is lifted up, since it is lived as part of a relationship with
Christ and as an offering to God. The glory of God is the living man
(cf. 1 Cor 10:31). And the life of man is the vision of God.

From the beginning Christians were clearly conscious of this
radical newness which the Eucharist brings to human life. The faithful
immediately perceived the profound influence of the eucharistic celebration on their manner of life. Saint Ignatius of Antioch expressed this
truth when he called Christians "those who have attained a new hope,"
and described them as "those living in accordance with the Lord's Day"
(*iuxta dominicam viventes*). This phrase of the great Antiochene martyr
highlights the connection between the reality of the Eucharist and
everyday Christian life. The Christians' customary practice of gathering on the first day after the Sabbath to celebrate the resurrection of

Christ—according to the account of Saint Justin Martyr—is also what defines the form of a life renewed by an encounter with Christ. Saint Ignatius' phrase—"living in accordance with the Lord's Day"—also emphasizes that this holy day becomes paradigmatic for every other day of the week. Indeed, it is defined by something more than the simple suspension of one's ordinary activities, a sort of parenthesis in one's usual daily rhythm. Christians have always experienced this day as the first day of the week, since it commemorates the radical newness brought by Christ. Sunday is thus the day when Christians rediscover the eucharistic form which their lives are meant to have. "Living in accordance with the Lord's Day" means living in the awareness of the liberation brought by Christ and making our lives a constant self-offering to God, so that his victory may be fully revealed to all humanity through a profoundly renewed existence.

Conscious of this new vital principle which the Eucharist imparts to the Christian, the Synod Fathers reaffirmed the importance of the Sunday obligation for all the faithful, viewing it as a wellspring of authentic freedom enabling them to live each day in accordance with what they celebrated on "the Lord's Day." The life of faith is endangered when we lose the desire to share in the celebration of the Eucharist and its commemoration of the paschal victory. Participating in the Sunday liturgical assembly with all our brothers and sisters, with whom we form one body in Jesus Christ, is demanded by our Christian conscience and at the same time it forms that conscience. To lose a sense of Sunday as the Lord's Day, a day to be sanctified, is symptomatic of the loss of an authentic sense of Christian freedom, the freedom of the children of God. Here some observations made by my venerable predecessor John Paul II in his Apostolic Letter *Dies Domini* continue to have great value. Speaking of the various dimensions of the Christian celebration of Sunday, he said that it is *Dies Domini* with regard to the work of creation, *Dies Christi* as the day of the new creation and the Risen Lord's gift of the Holy Spirit, *Dies Ecclesiae* as the day on which the Christian community gathers for the celebration, and *Dies hominis* as the day of joy, rest and fraternal charity.

Sunday thus appears as the primordial holy day, when all believers, wherever they are found, can become heralds and guardians of the true meaning of time. It gives rise to the Christian meaning of life and a new way of experiencing time, relationships, work, life and death. On the Lord's Day, then, it is fitting that Church groups should organize, around Sunday Mass, the activities of the Christian community: social gatherings, programs for the faith formation of children, young people and adults, pilgrimages, charitable works, and different moments of prayer. For the sake of these important values – while recognizing that Saturday evening, beginning with First Vespers, is already a part of Sunday and a time when the Sunday obligation can be fulfilled—we need to remember that it is Sunday itself that is meant to be kept holy, lest it end up as a day "empty of God."

Finally, it is particularly urgent nowadays to remember that the day of the Lord is also a day of rest from work. It is greatly to be hoped that this fact will also be recognized by civil society, so that individuals can be permitted to refrain from work without being penalized. Christians, not without reference to the meaning of the Sabbath in the Jewish tradition, have seen in the Lord's Day a day of rest from their daily exertions. This is highly significant, *for it relativizes work* and directs it to the person: work is for man and not man for work. It is easy to see how this actually protects men and women, emancipating them from a possible form of enslavement. As I have had occasion to say, "work is of fundamental importance to the fulfilment of the human being and to the development of society. Thus, it must always be organized and carried out with full respect for human dignity and must always serve the common good. At the same time, it is indispensable that people not allow themselves to be enslaved by work or to idolize it, claiming to find in it the ultimate and definitive meaning of life." It is on the day consecrated to God that men and women come to understand the meaning of their lives and also of their work.

QUESTIONS FOR REVIEW

1. What is the sin of idolatry?
2. What are three different ways we can violate the First Command-ment? Name them and describe them.
3. What are three different ways we can take the Lord's name in vain? Why is it important to honor God's name?
4. Why does God command us to rest on the Sabbath?
5. Why do Christians celebrate the Sabbath rest on Sunday instead of Saturday?

QUESTIONS FOR DISCUSSION

1. What are the idols in your life? What people or things have you ever put before God?
2. How commonly do you hear people taking the Lord's name in vain? Why do you think this is?
3. What does your Sunday typically look like? Why does it look like this? Is there anything you could change about it to make it more centered on God and restful?

Chapter 2

THE FOURTH AND FIFTH COMMANDMENTS

The Fourth Commandment: Honor Your Father and Your Mother

The first three commandments highlight our responsibilities toward God. The Fourth Commandment begins to concentrate on our relations to our neighbors, starting with our parents.

The Nature and Importance of Family

Our parents have given us the greatest of gifts: our life. Without them, we wouldn't exist. It doesn't matter if our parents are saints or sinners, we still owe our life to them, and that debt comes with obligations . . . and blessings. The Fourth Commandment is the only commandment with a blessing attached to it:

> Honor your father and your mother, that your days may be long in the land which the LORD your God gives you. (Exod 20:12)

In the ancient Jewish tradition, it was especially important to honor your father and mother because through them, you possessed not only natural life, but also a place in God's covenant with Israel. If you were born into the Israelite family, you belonged to God's Chosen People.

Once Jesus came, blood no longer determined our place in God's covenant family. Through his Son, God extended his covenant to all the nations (see Mark 3:34). Baptism and life in Jesus became the means of participating in God's covenant and receiving the gift of supernatural life. Jesus' coming, however, does not end the importance of the family; rather, it perfects it.

Since the beginning of human history, marriage existed as a natural sacrament. It was the means by which men and women gave themselves to each other in a fruitful, faithful, and enduring way. Also, through the families made by marriage, society was established and flourished. Marriage and the family are the building blocks of civilization. They are, the Catechism says, "the *original cell of social life*" (CCC 2207).

In the New Covenant the natural institution of marriage is taken up and made a sacrament. It becomes a source of grace for the spouses, helping them to love each other, raise up children, and serve Jesus through his Church. The graces of this sacrament, not surprisingly, come with responsibilities. Those responsibilities entail the care and fidelity the spouses give to each other; the obligation to be open to new life and provide both material and spiritual care for the children they welcome; and to be an epicenter of Christ's work in the world. The family is not meant to be closed in on itself. Rather, it's meant to open itself to the world, bringing Jesus' message of love and hope to all people:

> The family has the mission to guard, reveal and communicate love, and this is a living reflection of and a real sharing in God's love for humanity and the love of Christ the Lord for the Church His bride.[1]

In the Sacrament of Marriage, the spouses increase membership in the Church, serve as the first place for passing on the faith (this why the

---

[1] John Paul II, Apostolic Exhortation on the Role of the Christian Family in the Modern World *Familiaris Consortio* (November 22, 1981), §17.

home is called the domestic Church), and model Christ's relationship to the Church for the community (Eph 5:21–33). Essentially, the family forms a microcosm of the Church, as it is a unified community of faith, hope, and love. The family echoes the communion between the Father, Son, and Holy Spirit.

The Requirements of the Fourth Commandment

First and foremost, obeying the Fourth Commandment requires us to honor and love our parents. We must recognize our debt to them and express our gratitude for all they have done for us. It also requires that we obey them for as long as we remain in their care. As the Catechism says: "As long as a child lives at home with his parents, the child should obey his parents in all that they ask of him when it is for his good or that of the family" (CCC 2217).

Our obedience, of course, only goes so far. When we are older and living on our own, we aren't obliged to obey our parents. Likewise, if our parents ask us to do something that is sinful, we aren't obliged to obey them in that case either. Regardless, no matter what they ask of us or when they ask it of us, we are always obliged to show our parents respect. This respect is shown in words—how we speak to and about them—and how we demonstrate love and care for them throughout their life, including caring for their bodies and souls as they age or grow ill. Providing for their material needs and for their spiritual needs is a duty of honor.

Although obedience often has a bad reputation in the modern world, the Church sees the question differently. This, as the Catechism explains, is because "The divine fatherhood is the source of human fatherhood [Cf. *Eph* 314]; this is the foundation of the honor owed to parents" (CCC 2214). This applies to more than just parents. The Church believes that all legitimate authority derives its authority from God's own authority. Thus, as long as the authority is just, our obedience to that authority (including our parents) is obedience to God (CCC 2238).

Second, the reason God has established legitimate authorities, including our parents, is to protect the common good (or the good of the family). Therefore, to obey legitimate authority contributes to peace, justice, and human flourishing (including our own). Again, of course, this presumes that the authority commands what is true and good. We are not obliged to obey unjust authority.

In the familial context, children aren't the only ones with responsibilities. Parents owe children something as well. They must love their children (and avoid all hatred and ill will), help them in all their needs (providing food, shelter, clothing, sleep, and care), and see to their children's education (both physical and spiritual) (CCC 2221–2231).

While the Fourth Commandment deals primarily with families, it doesn't deal exclusively with families. It also calls us to honor all those to whom we are indebted for our existence. This includes our parents and grandparents, as well as our country and the Church. Accordingly, we should show reverence (honor) to our relatives, civil authorities, the Church's leaders, and the saints, obeying every just request of our family, every just law of our society (from traffic laws to taxes), and every just regulation of our Church.

We're also called to participate in society through these institutions—to contribute to the good of society through family life, work, service to our parish, voting, and involvement in other local and civic institutions (CCC 2239). In turn, civil and Church authorities have responsibilities to us, whom they serve. They must exercise their authority justly and for the common good (2235–2237).

In all this, the Catechism says:

> The fourth commandment *illuminates other relationships in society.* In our brothers and sisters we see the children of our parents; in our cousins, the descendants of our ancestors; in our fellow citizens, the children of our country; in the baptized, the children of our mother the Church; in every human person, a son or daughter of the One who wants to be called "our Father." In this way our relationships with our neighbors are recognized as personal in character. The neighbor is not a "unit" in the

human collective; he is "someone" who by his known origins deserves particular attention and respect. (CCC 2212)

The Fifth Commandment: You Shall Not Kill

The Fifth Commandment continues God's guidance for how humans should interact with each other, but unlike the first four commandments, it is a negative commandment, meaning it doesn't command us to do something. Rather, it commands us to not do something: You shall not kill.

The principal good protected by the Fifth Commandment is the good of the human person; it orders us to respect life in all its stages and situations. As we discussed earlier, every single human person possesses an absolute dignity that is not dependent on any other human person. No human being—no ruler, no employer, no boyfriend or girlfriend—gives us our dignity. Rather, our dignity comes purely from the fact that we are created by God, loved by God, and called by God to supernatural happiness. We are made in his image. Nothing we do, nothing someone else can do, and nothing that can happen to us can take away that dignity.

The intentional killing of an innocent human being is an outright failure to recognize a person's dignity. It's also a grave sin against God, who made that person and loves that person. Murder is always contrary to the virtue of justice. This includes not just random gang killings or murders motivated by passion, revenge, power, anger, lust, pride, envy, and greed, but also abortion, euthanasia, and embryonic stem cell research (CCC 2270–2279).

This doesn't mean that taking another person's life is always and everywhere sinful. Sacred Scripture outlines exactly what the Fifth Commandment requires: in Exodus 23:7, God says, "do not slay the innocent and the righteous." The same restrictions do not apply to those actively attempting to do us grave and bodily harm. The Church teaches that we have a right to protect our own life, and recognizes that this could result in the attacker's death. Taking the attacker's life is not the goal—the goal is protecting our life. And that makes a difference.[2]

This also holds true for the defense of another person. Each of us has a grave responsibility to defend the lives of those in our care. This applies to parents and also to leaders of a country (CCC 2312–2317). When defending others, though, (like when we're defending ourselves), we're called to use the minimum amount of force necessary to succeed. To be unnecessarily violent and cruel, or to enjoy harming another person, is just as much a violation of the Fifth Commandment as outright murder.

The death penalty is another example of legitimate killing. The Church has long taught that legitimate authorities have the right and duty to inflict punishment upon an offender. This punishment is not only what is due to the guilty party, but it also protects society physically and morally. Nevertheless, just as individuals are not allowed to use excessive force or harm to protect themselves, neither is the state. If there is a way to punish the offender and protect society without exercising the death penalty, the state is obliged to use it (CCC 2667).

The Fifth Commandment is not only concerned with preserving the physical lives of the innocent, but also with preserving bodily integrity. Kidnapping and hostage-taking, physical and mental torture, and dangerous experiments on human subjects are all threats to a person's bodily integrity (2292–2301).

Likewise, in the New Covenant, Jesus expands the Fifth Commandment even further:

> You have heard that it was said to the men of old, "You shall not kill; and whoever kills shall be liable to judgment." But I say to you that every one who is angry with his brother shall be liable to judgment; whoever insults his brother shall be liable to the council, and whoever says, "You fool!" shall be liable to the hell of fire. (Matt 5:21)

So, the problem is not simply murdering one's neighbor. The anger that gives birth to murder, as well as many other sins, is the real problem

---

[2] Aquinas, ST II-II, q. 64, a. 7.

(CCC 2302). Jesus, therefore, condemns unjust anger and anger that overrules our ability to think.

The prohibitions of the Fifth Commandment also include how we treat ourselves. It prohibits killing ourselves, both literally and metaphorically. This is why the Catholic Church has always condemned suicide (CCC 2280–2283). Our lives are not ours to take; they belong to God. Of course, suicide is not always freely chosen on account of social coercion or mental problems, so nobody but God fully knows a person's culpability when they commit suicide. Nevertheless, suicide is still always wrong. It is also cruel, as it wounds those left behind in devastating and lasting ways. It is absolutely never a good or loving thing to do.

Metaphorically speaking, the Fifth Commandment calls us to care for our bodies, avoiding things which harm them, including cutting one's self, taking dangerous drugs or an excess of alcohol or tobacco, undereating or overeating (CCC 2288–2291). The Fifth Commandment's prohibition on self-harm also includes medical procedures that harm our functional bodily integrity. Thus, we cannot take a perfectly healthy and functioning body part, organ, or organ system and destroy it, as happens in vasectomies and tubal ligations. That is violence against ourselves (CCC 2312–2317).

SELECTED READING
John Paul II, Encyclical Letter on the Value and Inviolability of Human Life *Evangelium Vitae* (March 25, 1995), nos. 58–62

Among all the crimes which can be committed against life, procured abortion has characteristics making it particularly serious and deplorable. The Second Vatican Council defines abortion, together with infanticide, as an "unspeakable crime."

But today, in many people's consciences, the perception of its gravity has become progressively obscured. The acceptance of abortion in the popular mind, in behaviour and even in law itself, is a telling sign of an extremely dangerous crisis of the moral sense, which is becoming more and more incapable of distinguishing between good and evil, even when the fundamental right to life is at stake. Given such a grave situation, we need now more than ever to have the courage to look the truth in the eye and to call things by their proper name, without yielding to convenient compromises or to the temptation of self-deception. In this regard the reproach of the Prophet is extremely straightforward: "Woe to those who call evil good and good evil, who put darkness for light and light for darkness" (Is 5:20). Especially in the case of abortion there is a widespread use of ambiguous terminology, such as "interruption of pregnancy," which tends to hide abortion's true nature and to attenuate its seriousness in public opinion. Perhaps this linguistic phenomenon is itself a symptom of an uneasiness of conscience. But no word has the power to change the reality of things: procured abortion is the deliberate and direct killing, by whatever means it is carried out, of a human being in the initial phase of his or her existence, extending from conception to birth.

The moral gravity of procured abortion is apparent in all its truth if we recognize that we are dealing with murder and, in particular, when we consider the specific elements involved. The one eliminated is a human being at the very beginning of life. No one more absolutely innocent could be imagined. In no way could this human being ever be considered an aggressor, much less an unjust aggressor! He or she is weak, defenseless, even to the point of lacking that minimal form of defense consisting in the poignant power of a newborn baby's cries and tears. The unborn child is totally entrusted to the protection and care of the woman carrying him or her in the womb. And yet sometimes it is precisely the mother herself who makes the decision and asks for the child to be eliminated, and who then goes about having it done.

It is true that the decision to have an abortion is often tragic and painful for the mother, insofar as the decision to rid herself of the fruit of conception is not made for purely selfish reasons or out of convenience, but out of a desire to protect certain important values such as her own health or a decent standard of living for the other members of the family. Sometimes it is feared that the child to be born would live in such conditions that it would be better if the birth did not take place. Nevertheless, these reasons and others like them, however serious and tragic, can never justify the deliberate killing of an innocent human being.

As well as the mother, there are often other people too who decide upon the death of the child in the womb. In the first place, the father of the child may be to blame, not only when he directly pressures the woman to have an abortion, but also when he indirectly encourages such a decision on her part by leaving her alone to face the problems of pregnancy: in this way the family is thus mortally wounded and profaned in its nature as a community of love and in its vocation to be the "sanctuary of life." Nor can one overlook the pressures which sometimes come from the wider family circle and from friends. Sometimes the woman is subjected to such strong pressure that she feels psychologically forced to have an abortion: certainly in this case moral responsibility lies particularly with those who have directly or indirectly obliged her to have an abortion. Doctors and nurses are also responsible, when they place at the service of death skills which were acquired for promoting life.

But responsibility likewise falls on the legislators who have promoted and approved abortion laws, and, to the extent that they have a say in the matter, on the administrators of the health-care centres where abortions are performed. A general and no less serious responsibility lies with those who have encouraged the spread of an attitude of sexual permissiveness and a lack of esteem for motherhood, and with those who should have ensured—but did not—effective family and social policies in support of families, especially larger families and those with particular financial and educational needs. . . .

Human life is sacred and inviolable at every moment of existence, including the initial phase which precedes birth. All human beings, from their mothers' womb, belong to God who searches them and knows them, who forms them and knits them together with his own hands, who gazes on them when they are tiny shapeless embryos and already sees in them the adults of tomorrow whose days are numbered and whose vocation is even now written in the "book of life" (cf. Ps 139:1, 13–16). There too, when they are still in their mothers' womb—as many passages of the Bible bear witness—they are the personal objects of God's loving and fatherly providence. . . .

Throughout Christianity's two thousand year history, this same doctrine has been constantly taught by the Fathers of the Church and by her Pastors and Doctors. Even scientific and philosophical discussions about the precise moment of the infusion of the spiritual soul have never given rise to any hesitation about the moral condemnation of abortion.

The more recent Papal Magisterium has vigorously reaffirmed this common doctrine. Pius XI in particular, in his Encyclical *Casti Connubii*, rejected the specious justifications of abortion. Pius XII excluded all direct abortion, i.e., every act tending directly to destroy human life in the womb "whether such destruction is intended as an end or only as a means to an end." John XXIII reaffirmed that human life is sacred because "from its very beginning it directly involves God's creative activity." The Second Vatican Council, as mentioned earlier, sternly condemned abortion: "From the moment of its conception life must be guarded with the greatest care, while abortion and infanticide are unspeakable crimes." . . .

Therefore, by the authority which Christ conferred upon Peter and his Successors, in communion with the Bishops—who on various occasions have condemned abortion and who in the aforementioned consultation, albeit dispersed throughout the world, have shown unanimous agreement concerning this doctrine—I declare that direct abortion, that is, abortion willed as an end or as a means, always constitutes a grave moral disorder, since it is the deliberate killing of an innocent human being. This doctrine is based upon the natural law and upon the written Word of God, is transmitted by the Church's Tradition and taught by the ordinary and universal Magisterium.

No circumstance, no purpose, no law whatsoever can ever make licit an act which is intrinsically illicit, since it is contrary to the Law of God which is written in every human heart, knowable by reason itself, and proclaimed by the Church.

QUESTIONS FOR REVIEW

1. What three obligations does marriage entail?
2. Under the Fourth Commandment, what are parents' obligations to their children? What are children's obligations to their parents?
3. What theological truth about each of us is at the heart of the commandment "Thou shalt not kill"?
4. How does the Fifth Commandment apply to how we should treat ourselves?
5. What sin is at the root of murder?

QUESTIONS FOR DISCUSSION

1. Is it difficult for you to honor your parents, guardians, or other authority figures? Why or why not?
2. Why do you think our society is complicit in some kinds of murder: abortion, assisted suicide, the death penalty? Why is this still wrong?
3. What are some practical things you can do to encourage people to better respect all human life?

Chapter 3

THE SIXTH COMMANDMENT

The Sixth Commandment: You Shall Not Commit Adultery

On Mount Sinai, God forbade his people from committing adultery—from being unfaithful to one's spouse. But 1,500 years later, Jesus sternly warned his followers that being sexually faithful to one's spouse wasn't enough to fulfill the Sixth Commandment. "You have heard that it was said, 'You shall not commit adultery'" he said. "But I say to you that every one who looks at a woman lustfully has already committed adultery with her in his heart" (Matt 5:27–28).

Jesus' words cut straight to the heart of human sexuality, targeting not just damaging sexual behavior, but also the deadly attitude that gives rise to every form of damaging sexual behavior: lust. Accordingly, in the 20 centuries since he spoke those words, the Church has read the Sixth Commandment as an injunction to live the gift of sexuality in truth and freedom. The Church's understanding of what truth and freedom mean in the context of sexuality, however, is radically different from the culture's understanding.

The Gift of Human Sexuality

The Church, unlike the culture, recognizes that sexuality is written into the story of man's creation. Of all the gifts God has bestowed on the human person, sexuality is, in a certain sense, the most fundamental. It is who we are: a man or a woman. It shapes how we live and love. Above all, it reveals that for which we were made—that we are creatures created for union, for communion, in this life with another human being and in eternity with God himself.

In his reflections on human sexuality, St. John Paul II beautifully unpacks how the love of man and woman, together in marriage, resembles, in a way, the communion of the Holy Trinity. In the Trinity, each Divine Person gives himself wholly and completely to the other. Their union is eternal and unbreakable. It is also fruitful, generating love and life. This life of shared life-giving love that subsists eternally within the Trinity is echoed by the love of man and woman in marriage, a love that is free, faithful, and fruitful. John Paul II calls this "the spousal meaning of the body."[1]

As John Paul II explained in his *Theology of the Body*, men and women are made for each other. Our bodies testify to this. They are like corresponding puzzle pieces, created to fit together and work together. Men's bodies and women's bodies only make sense in light of each other. And when they come together, in the right ways and times, they do what *only* the body of a man and a woman can do together: they create new human life.

The same differences between men and women that make it possible for new life to come into being are equally fruitful on a spiritual level. The Church teaches that men and women are equal in dignity, but she also recognizes that equal doesn't mean the same. The differences between men and women go beyond skin deep. In fact, according to St. John Paul II, the differences in our bodies "constitute, so to speak, two diverse ways of 'being a body' that are proper to the human nature in the unity of [the divine] image."[2]

Essentially, the Church teaches that men and women possess our

---

[1] John Paul II, *Man and Woman He Created Them: A Theology of the Body* (hereafter cited as TOB), trans. Michael Waldstein (Boston: Pauline Books and Media, 2006), 13:2.

[2] see TOB, 14:4: "By exclaiming ['she is flesh from my flesh and bone from my bones'], [Adam] seems to say, *Look, a body that expresses the 'person!'*"

human nature in different but complementary ways. These differences help each sex perfect the other. We are better together than we are apart. This complementarity of the sexes underlines once more the truth that we are not made for ourselves. We are made for communion with another. St. John Paul II explained it this way:

> Femininity in some way finds itself before masculinity, while masculinity confirms itself through femininity. . . . The presence of the feminine element, next to the masculine and together with it, signifies an enrichment for man in the whole perspective of his history, including the history of salvation.[3]

Sexuality is indeed one of the greatest gifts God has given us. Through the act of giving ourselves to another—body and soul—we become more truly and fully ourselves. "Man becomes an image of God not so much in the moment of solitude," John Paul II wrote, "as in the moment of communion."[4]

Not surprisingly, though, a gift with such great potential also comes with tremendous responsibilities. Just as our sexuality can be a source of joy and blessing when we use it rightly, it also can be a source of tremendous pain and suffering—to us and others—when we use it wrongly.

The Right Use of the Gift

The very nature of sexual intimacy demands that it be used in one context and one context alone: marriage. This is a truth we can discover simply through the use of reason.

From a biological perspective, sexual relations have two primary physical consequences. The first is babies. When a healthy man and a healthy woman of child-bearing age give themselves to each other, the normal result is a baby. Maybe not the first time, but eventually. Babies are great gifts, but they also come with a lifetime of responsibilities. Chil-

---

[3]   TOB, 10:1.
[4]   TOB, 9:3.

dren need parents—not for just one month or one year, but for decades. The parents, in turn, need support. Caring for a child is a great undertaking, and not one we're meant to carry out alone. It takes two to make a baby, and ideally, it takes two to raise a baby. Which is where the second physical effect of sexual relations comes in: bonding.

When you give your body to another—when you cuddle, kiss, and are physically intimate—a hormone called oxytocin is released. The more intimate you are, the more oxytocin flows. This is also the same hormone released in a new mother when she begins breastfeeding her baby. Called "the bonding hormone," oxytocin binds you emotionally to the person you have been with. It creates a chemical attachment between two people that makes it difficult to walk away from each other. This helps new moms want to care for their babies—no matter how much they cry and deprive their moms of sleep. And it helps men and women stay together so they can raise the child they've created together. It doesn't force people to stay together; our experience tells us that. But it does make it difficult to separate. This is one of the reasons why it's so hard to get over someone if you break up. A real, physical connection remains.

The ends of sexuality—babies and bonding, or procreation and unity—make clear the proper context of sexual relations: marriage. Marriage is the only relationship in which the inherent goals of sex can be met in a unified and full way. It is a lifelong conjugal relationship ordered toward spousal unity and the procreation and education of children— toward bonding and babies. The two match perfectly. It also is the only relationship in which a person makes a whole gift of themselves to another person—a gift that involves their body and their soul and lasts a lifetime.

The virtue of chastity makes this proper ordering of our sexuality possible.

The Virtue of Chastity

People often think of chastity as simply not having sex, but that's not accurate. Chastity is actually the virtue that moderates our desire for sexual activity and integrates our sexuality with our whole person, conforming our desires to the true and the good (CCC 2337). In short, chastity makes us free from acting on our every sexual impulse, allowing us instead to freely interact with others as people and not as objects of sexual desire. As such, chastity is not simply for those who are unmarried. It's for everyone—priests and religious, married people and single people. This means that how people practice chastity depends on their state in life.

For those called to religious or consecrated life, chastity means celibacy (never marrying) and continence (not having sexual relations). Religious brothers and sisters refrain from marriage and sexual relations in order to give themselves wholeheartedly to God. In effect, they begin to live now the life the saints live in heaven, a life in which "they neither marry nor are given in marriage, but are like angels in heaven" (Mark 12:25). Celibacy is a sign of the coming kingdom.

For the married person, chastity is expressed in a conjugal relationship. Within marriage, sex is not merely tolerated; it's celebrated. Marital sexuality is a good and holy thing, which brings new life into the world and unites the couple more closely together. This doesn't mean that anything goes in marriage, though.

Married sexuality has to respect the ends of both marriage and sex: unity and procreation. So, if one spouse treats the other as an object of lust and seeks to use them sexually in a way that is contrary to the good of the whole person, that violates the end of unity and is a sin against chastity. Likewise, if a couple uses artificial contraception or surgically destroys their fertility, they sin against chastity by violating the end of procreation. They are constructing an artificial barrier to prevent the natural and right end of both marriage and sex: babies. Pope Paul VI explained this in his encyclical, *Humanae Vitae*.

> Men rightly observe that a conjugal act imposed on one's partner without regard to his or her condition or personal and reasonable wishes in the matter, is no true act of love, and therefore offends the moral order in its particular application to the intimate relationship of husband and wife. If they further reflect, they must also recognize that an act of mutual love which impairs the

capacity to transmit life which God the Creator, through specific laws, has built into it, frustrates His design which constitutes the norm of marriage, and contradicts the will of the Author of life. Hence to use this divine gift while depriving it, even if only partially, of its meaning and purpose, is equally repugnant to the nature of man and of woman, and is consequently in opposition to the plan of God and His holy will.[5]

Finally, for single people, chastity requires continence and abstinence. It requires striving to see each person as an image of God—not an object for our own desire—and refraining both from sexual activities that are proper to marriage and those activities that arouse desire and can make saying no to sex difficult.

Sexual activity outside of marriage always does violence to the sexual act and the human person. It does violence to the gift of sex by denying its purpose of bonding two people together for a lifetime. It also does violence to the gift of procreation by creating the possible conditions for new life between two people who are not committed to each other and the possible child. When contraception is involved, that violence is compounded. The use of contraception denies sex's procreative purpose—of bringing new life into the world—and it denies its unitive purpose by allowing people to use each other for pleasure without making a full gift of themselves—a gift that involves their whole self, including their fertility. Sex outside of marriage is a charade of the real, total, and committed self-gift that takes place only within marriage.

Sins Against the Sixth Commandment

Just as all are called to live chastely, the sins against chastity can occur in any form of life—religious, married, or single. As Jesus explained in the Gospel of Matthew, the root of these sins is lust.

---

[5] Paul VI, Encyclical Letter on the Regulation of Birth *Humanae Vitae* (July 25, 1968), §13.

Lust is the vice of disordered desire for sexual pleasure (CCC 2351). We are lustful when we nurse a desire for sex that is unreasonable, or is contrary to chastity, the dignity of the human person, and the nature of sex itself.

Lust, which is itself sinful, can lead us into any number of sins, starting with fornication, which is sex outside of marriage (1 Cor 6:18; CCC 2353).

Masturbation is another sin against the Sixth Commandment (CCC 2352). Like fornication, it is a rejection of the purposes of sexual activity. It denies both the unitive aspect and the procreative aspect of sex, reducing sex to a solitary act for personal pleasure, not a gift from God meant to bring the grace of union and new life into the world. In this, it not only does violence to sex, but to the human person as well, reducing us to our sexual appetites and making it more difficult for us to truly give ourselves to another and value the other for who they are and not for the pleasure sexual relations with them can give.

Pornography comes with similar dangers: it denies the twofold purpose of sex and violates the dignity of the human person (CCC 2354). It also carries the additional gravity of violating the dignity of the people involved in the production of the pornographic material. If we consume pornography, we reduce those involved to objects to be used for our personal pleasure, and we also contribute to all the evils surrounding the pornography industry: prostitution, sex slaves, drug abuse, and the exploitation of others. Moreover, pornography itself has been shown to be highly addictive.[6] It diminishes our freedom and puts the pornography, not us, in control of our sexuality.

Rape and Prostitution are likewise sins against the Sixth Commandment (2355–2356). Both strip sexuality of the heart of its beauty—the free gift of one's self to another. Violence, force, and money have no place in the sexual act. The sin of rape is compounded when it is against children, or when it takes place within the family, which is the sin of incest

---

[6] See Todd Love, et al., "Neuroscience of Internet Pornography Addiction: A Review and Update," *Behavioral Sciences* 5, no. 3 (2015): 388–433, https://doi.org/10.3390/bs5030388.

(CCC 2388–2389).

Homosexual activity is also wrong for the same reasons fornication, masturbation, and contraception are wrong: it violates the unitive and procreative ends of sexual activity.

As the Catechism of the Catholic Church explains:

> Basing itself on Sacred Scripture, which presents homosexual acts as acts of grave depravity [Cf. *Gen* 191–29; *Rom* 124–27; *1 Cor* 6:10; *1 Tim* 1:10], tradition has always declared that "homosexual acts are intrinsically disordered" [CDF, *Persona humana* 8]. They are contrary to the natural law. They close the sexual act to the gift of life. They do not proceed from a genuine affective and sexual complementarity. Under no circumstances can they be approved. (CCC 2357)

The Catechism then continues:

> The number of men and women who have deep-seated homosexual tendencies is not negligible. This inclination, which is objectively disordered, constitutes for most of them a trial. They must be accepted with respect, compassion, and sensitivity. Every sign of unjust discrimination in their regard should be avoided. These persons are called to fulfill God's will in their lives and, if they are Christians, to unite to the sacrifice of the Lord's Cross the difficulties they may encounter from their condition. (CCC 2358)

It's important to note here that the Church doesn't teach that it's sinful to experience feelings of attraction for members of the same sex. Feelings, in and of themselves, aren't sinful; it's what we do with those feelings—whether we nurse them and act on them or not—that matters. Each of us is responsible for our actions, not for our attractions.

It's also important to understand that in the eyes of the Church and in the eyes of Jesus, sexual orientation as the culture understands it is not essential to the true identity of the person. As Christians, our primary identity is found in Jesus: each of us is a unique, unrepeatable, beloved child of God. Who we are sexually attracted to is one *element* of our identity. It's not *who we are*.

Infidelity and spousal abandonment are two more ways couples can violate chastity and the Sixth Commandment within marriage (CCC 2380–2386). Both sins are rooted in the truth that sexual intercourse is only virtuous within marriage and renews the marital commitment made in the marriage ceremony. The spouses repeat their vows with their bodies every time they make love. This requires, on account of their freely taken vows and the logic of the sexual act, that the spouses be faithful to each other and that marriage be monogamous. Hence, both polygamy and adultery are also contrary to the sexual act and the meaning of marriage.

Likewise, marriage between the baptized is indissoluble (CCC 1646). Jesus himself explicitly states this:

> Now I say this to you: anyone who divorces his wife, except for unchastity, and marries another, commits adultery. (Matt 19:9)

Divorce itself is not necessarily sinful. There are occasions where the safety of one of the spouses or the children require separation. Likewise, a person who has been abandoned by their spouse against their will has committed no sin. And sometimes something was wrong with the marriage to start with; one of the spouses was forced into the marriage or was not capable of making a free gift of themselves at the time of the vows because of some impediment (such as substance abuse or mental illness). Catholics in these circumstances are able to obtain an annulment, which recognizes that a valid sacramental marriage never existed in the first place.

So, where does the sin come in? First, if an annulment is not sought and granted and a person remarries, that second marriage is adulterous (Matt 19:9). The spouse, in the eyes of God, remains married to another, so no valid second union can exist. Likewise, if a real marriage does exist and one spouse abandons the other out of selfishness or lust for another, that is a sin. Spouses vow to remain faithful to each other and support each other "until death do us part." They make that vow, solemnly, before God.

Since the marital relationship and the sexual act are both ordered toward procreation and the raising of children, those who suffer from infertility suffer greatly. It strikes a blow to the very heart of their marital and sexual relationship. To alleviate this suffering, secular society offers the manipulation of the body and the person in the forms of artificial procreation, such as in-vitro fertilization (IVF), intrauterine insemination (IUI), and surrogacy.

The Church rejects these methods as evil means used to achieve a good end. IVF, IUI, and surrogacy all treat children as a commodity, not as gifts. They are expensive, invasive, and deprive the child of their right to be created in a loving act of union between a mother and a father. They also result in the creation of multiple embryos, who are routinely frozen and discarded when not implanted, and selectively aborted when they are implanted. Hundreds of thousands of small frozen human beings currently fill the warehouses of fertility clinics. The overwhelming majority of those children will never be born. They will never be given a chance for life. The Church recognizes the cruelty of creating life only to discard it, and calls people to instead seek more ethical treatments for infertility, including NaProTECHNOLOGY, which looks to heal the underlying causes of male and female infertility through sound medical science.

Openness to Life

Yet another way spouses can sin against the Sixth Commandment is through contraceptive sex. Both the logic of the sexual act and marriage requires that spouses be open to new life. Indeed, *Gaudium et Spes* says:

> Parents should regard as their proper mission the task of transmitting human life and educating those to whom it has been transmitted. They should realize that they are thereby cooperators with the love of God the Creator, and are, so to speak, the interpreters of that love.[7]

---

[7] Second Vatican Council, Pastoral Constitution on the Church in the Modern World

Does this mean that spouses must produce as many children as possible? No, not at all. Instead, the Church calls the faithful to prudently, generously, and continually discern the number of children God is calling them to have. As the Church sees it, the number of children we bear is not a once-and-done decision. It's a question to be asked perpetually during the childbearing years, as circumstances and desires change.

To both conceive and postpone conceiving, the Church supports the use of natural family planning (NFP). While there are many different methods of natural family planning, the practice itself is rooted in science and works with the natural cycles of a woman's body to track fertility. When a couple is striving to conceive, identifying the woman's fertile window and engaging in marital relations during her most fertile days increases their chances of having a baby. When a couple is trying to avoid conception, they use the fertile period as a time of abstinence.

NFP respects the inherent goals of the sexual act. It also recognizes that the decision to have or avoid another child is up to the couple. To make this decision well, the couple must communicate with each other and strive to make wise decisions about what is best for them as a couple and their family. Furthermore, NFP is radically pro-woman. It does not assume that women's bodies are diseased or broken, and that fertility itself is an illness. Lastly, it requires men and women to subordinate their sexual desires to what is good for the woman, the family, and the common good of society. Importantly, when used properly, natural family planning methods are as effective or more effective than artificial contraceptives such as the Pill, condoms, and other devices.[8]

Gaudium et Spes (December 7, 1965), §50.

[8] Crista B. Warniment, M.D., and Kirsten Hansen, M.D., "Is Natural Family Planning a Highly Effective Method of Birth Control? Yes: Natural Family Planning Is Highly Effective and Fulfilling," *American Family Physician* 86, n. 10 (November 15, 2012), https://www.aafp.org/afp/2012/1115/od1.html; Association of Reproductive Health Professionals, "Contraceptive Failure Rates," (June, 2014), http://www.arhp.org/Publications-and-Resources/Quick-Reference-Guide-for-Clinicians/choosing/failure-rates-table.

SELECTED READING
Francis, Post-Synodal Apostolic Exhortation on Love in the
Family *Amoris Laetitia* (March 19, 2016), nos. 150–152

All this brings us to the sexual dimension of marriage. God himself
created sexuality, which is a marvelous gift to his creatures. If this gift
needs to be cultivated and directed, it is to prevent the "impoverish-
ment of an authentic value." Saint John Paul II rejected the claim that
the Church's teaching is "a negation of the value of human sexuality,"
or that the Church simply tolerates sexuality "because it is necessary
for procreation." Sexual desire is not something to be looked down
upon, and "and there can be no attempt whatsoever to call into question its necessity."

To those who fear that the training of the passions and of sexuality detracts from the spontaneity of sexual love, Saint John Paul II
replied that human persons are "called to full and mature spontaneity in their relationships," a maturity that "is the gradual fruit of a discernment of the impulses of one's own heart." This calls for discipline
and self-mastery, since every human person "must learn, with perseverance and consistency, the meaning of his or her body." Sexuality
is not a means of gratification or entertainment; it is an interpersonal
language wherein the other is taken seriously, in his or her sacred
and inviolable dignity. As such, "the human heart comes to participate, so to speak, in another kind of spontaneity." In this context,
the erotic appears as a specifically human manifestation of sexuality.
It enables us to discover "the nuptial meaning of the body and the
authentic dignity of the gift." In his catecheses on the theology of the
body, Saint John Paul II taught that sexual differentiation not only
is "a source of fruitfulness and procreation," but also possesses "the
capacity of expressing love: that love precisely in which the human
person becomes a gift." A healthy sexual desire, albeit closely joined
to a pursuit of pleasure, always involves a sense of wonder, and for
that very reason can humanize the impulses.

In no way, then, can we consider the erotic dimension of love
simply as a permissible evil or a burden to be tolerated for the good

of the family. Rather, it must be seen as gift from God that enriches the relationship of the spouses. As a passion sublimated by a love respectful of the dignity of the other, it becomes a "pure, unadulterated affirmation" revealing the marvels of which the human heart is capable. In this way, even momentarily, we can feel that "life has turned out good and happy."

On the basis of this positive vision of sexuality, we can approach the entire subject with a healthy realism. It is, after all, a fact that sex often becomes depersonalized and unhealthy; as a result, "it becomes the occasion and instrument for self-assertion and the selfish satisfaction of personal desires and instincts." In our own day, sexuality risks being poisoned by the mentality of "use and discard." The body of the other is often viewed as an object to be used as long as it offers satisfaction, and rejected once it is no longer appealing. Can we really ignore or overlook the continuing forms of domination, arrogance, abuse, sexual perversion and violence that are the product of a warped understanding of sexuality? Or the fact that the dignity of others and our human vocation to love thus end up being less important than an obscure need to "find oneself"?

QUESTIONS FOR REVIEW

1. What does sexual difference reveal about the human person?
2. What are the two lasting physical consequences of sexual intimacy? How do they correspond to the two primary ends of marriage?
3. What is the virtue of chastity and how are people in different states in life called to practice this virtue?
4. What are five different ways we can break the Sixth Commandment? Why do these go against the gift of sexuality?
5. Who is harmed by the sin of viewing pornography?

QUESTIONS FOR DISCUSSION

1. What are some of the consequences you have seen of people misusing the gift of sexuality?

2. Have you ever been treated more like an object—as something to be used—than as a subject—as someone to be loved? How did that make you feel?
3. Do you think our culture has made an idol out of sex? If so, how and why?

Chapter 4

The Seventh through Tenth Commandments

The Seventh Commandment: You Shall Not Steal

"Don't take what doesn't belong to you," is one of the first lessons we learn as children. We know, from an early age, that sneaking food, "borrowing" our siblings toys, or taking something from a store is wrong. But why is it wrong? And are there any other types of stealing we need to avoid? To answer those questions, we first need to look at what the Church teaches about private property.

The Catholic Church has always taught that we have the right to private property so that we may provide for ourselves and our families (CCC 2211). This right, which is prior to civil law, is rooted in human nature—in the natural inclination to procreate, provide for, and educate children. It also is rooted in the doctrine of the universal destination of goods, which holds that God intended the world for the sustenance of all without distinction (CCC 2401).

At first glance, this can sound contradictory, with the doctrine of the universal destination of goods sounding a little like communism and seeming to undermine, not uphold, the right to private property. But that's not the case. First, the Church has long condemned communism as an economic system contrary to human nature and human dignity.[1] So, while the Church teaches that the earth and its resources are meant for all, she also teaches that this goal must be sought in a way that respects human nature, and that includes respecting the right to private property.

In other words, the Catholic Church holds both that the goods of the earth are destined for the sustenance of all *and* that natural law promotes private property as a way of meeting this end. This respects both the dignity of the human person and the principle of subsidiarity.[2] Accordingly, each of us is to consider our private property to be at the service of our brothers and sisters, and whoever among us has more property than we need should pass that property on to whomever it really belongs (i.e. the poor).

This is why the Church often says that the right to private property is not absolute. By this, she means the right to the use of one's property is not absolute; it must be used for the good of others. In a sense, property has a social mortgage on it. To have more than we need and not share it with others is an offense against justice. Likewise, to use property without any reference to the good of others is an offense against justice; it is a type of theft (CCC 2405). Catholics are called to use their property for the good of others, as stewards of God's providence.

> Man should regard the external things that he legitimately possesses not only as his own but also as common in the sense that they should be able to benefit not only him but also others. On the other hand, the right of having a share of earthly goods sufficient for oneself and one's family belongs to everyone. The Fathers and Doctors of the Church held this opinion, teaching that men are obliged to come to the relief of the poor and to do so not merely out of their superfluous goods.[3]

---

[1] See Leo XIII, Encyclical Letter on the Rights and Duties of Capital and Labor *Rerum Novarum* (May 15, 1891), §15.
[2] John Paul II, Encyclical Letter on the Hundredth Anniversary of Rerum Novarum *Centesimus Annus* (May 1, 1991), §48.
[3] *Gaudium et Spes*, §69.

Given that the Church supports a doctrine of private ownership, she logically claims that to take what belongs to another without his or her consent is wrong. It is directly prohibited by the Seventh Commandment. In our culture, this taking manifests in many different forms, from business fraud to paying unjust wages, unfair price manipulation, and price gouging. The command against stealing also includes prohibitions against work poorly done, tax evasion, forgery, and excessive expenses/wastefulness. When we do any of these things, we take, retain, or refuse to give another what belongs to them.

The Social Doctrine of the Church

The Church's teachings on the Seventh Commandment are intimately bound up with the Church's social doctrine, often referred to as Catholic Social Thought (CST). Fundamentally, CST is a subdiscipline of moral theology, which outlines a holistic Catholic vision, based on both revelation and reason, of a good human society. It arises from faith and the command to love one's neighbor, but reflects on realities of the social, economic, and cultural spheres. Because of its reliance on both revelation and reason, it contains both permanently valid principles and contingent judgments. That is to say, it contains teachings that never change and teachings that are pertinent to specific times and places.

Detailing the whole of CST is beyond the scope of this book. We do, however, need to at least understand its fundamental outline, because the ethical and moral questions we're covering here are bound up with the Church's larger vision for a virtuous society. In fact, individual and social ethics are so radically interconnected that one can't coherently believe in the Church's individual ethics (such as its sexual doctrine) without also believing in her social ethics, or vice-versa. As Pope Benedict XVI explained in his encyclical letter *Caritas in Veritate*, all of the Church's teachings are interconnected, with each one reinforcing and helping explain the other.

The book of nature is one and indivisible: it takes in not only the environment but also life, sexuality, marriage, the family, social relations: in a word, integral human development. Our duties towards the environment are linked to our duties towards the human person, considered in himself and in relation to others. It would be wrong to uphold one set of duties while trampling on the other. Herein lies a grave contradiction in our mentality and practice today: one which demeans the person, disrupts the environment and damages society.[4]

All Catholic Social Thought is rooted in three fundamental truths about the human person.

1. Humans are social creatures.

This means that we are made for communion—for family and friendship with others—and find our perfection not by "going it alone," but rather by living in society. Our first experience of this communion is in our family, which is the fundamental unit of society and exists as an institution prior to civil authority.[5] It is in the family that one first sees humanity's social nature.

Our social nature also reminds us that we are not fundamentally in competition with each other, nor is the good of one the detriment of the other. There is a real unity to the human community, such that what is right in light of the common good is the perfection of each part of society and the individual members.[6]

Because of this, the Church rejects *unfettered* capitalism (meaning a capitalist system with no checks upon it to ensure justice for all), because such a system is founded exclusively on competition, profit, and consumption.[7] Furthermore, such a system of capitalism can't meet all the needs of the human community and ultimately leaves many on the margins and

---

[4] Benedict XVI, Encylical Letter on Integral Human Development in Charity and Truth *Caritas in Veritate* (June 29, 2009), §51.

[5] *Rerum Novaruvm*, §12.

[6] *Caritatis in Veritate*, §7.

[7] *Rerum Novarum*, §3.

excluded.[8] Likewise, unfettered capitalism does not take seriously the doctrine of the unity of the human family, the common good, or solidarity—the Church's teaching that the human community is united and, in a very real sense, we are all our brother's keepers (Gen 4:9).

On the other hand, the Church also rejects economic systems that are a form of false collectivism, such as socialism or communism.[9] These systems are also contrary to human dignity and the right understanding of the human person, who is called to exercise initiative, creativity, responsibility, and ownership.

Economic and political systems such as fascism, which destroy both the family and intermediate institutions (such as the Church) are likewise contrary to Catholic teaching. Humans are not cogs in an impersonal economic and political machine. The economy exists for the human person, not the other way around. This is also true of work. CST teaches not only that employers owe their employees a living wage—a wage sufficient to support the family and one that takes people's needs into account—but also that work should be personal and meaningful.[10]

These types of false collectivism contravene the doctrine of subsidiarity, in which the Church teaches that each level of society (the state, intermediate institutions, and the family) should have its own responsibilities for the common good, and those responsibilities shouldn't be assumed by a higher level unless the lower cannot or will not perform its proper function.

Of course, the common good must really be common. This is why the Church opposes a serious gap between the rich and the poor, both within and between nations.[11] A serious gap between rich and poor means that the common good is being reserved for a few, so that the common good is not really common. Hence, the rich have a responsibility to not burden the poor, to aid them directly in times of need, and to establish

[8] *Centesimus Annus,* §34.

[9] *Rerum Novarum,* §4.

[10] John Paul II, Encyclical Letter on Human Work *Laborem Exercens* (September 14, 1981), §5.

[11] John XXIII, Encyclical Letter on Christianity and Social Progress *Mater et Magistra* (May 15, 1961), §150.

structures that allow people to rise out of poverty. Rich nations have the same obligation to poor nations. They also must not burden poor nations with unjust negotiations and must reform international relations so that poorer nations can participate and flourish. Finally, they must do this while respecting the poorer nations' culture and not simply exporting their own.[12]

2. Humans are made in the image of God.

As outlined earlier, this means that we have a rational and free nature and a fundamental and irrevocable dignity. Our rationality and freedom are perfected in virtue (which essentially means good moral habits). In a fundamental sense, CST is about how to live the virtues in society. Any social program that claims the only thing necessary to fix society is to fix its laws or social structures is contrary to Catholic teaching.

This is because the fundamental source of evil in society isn't bad laws; it's the human heart. It's the state of original sin in which we're all born and the concupiscence that infests our souls. The evil from the human heart can take on a concrete shape in structural sin—in bad laws and institutions—but that doesn't change its origin.[13] As such, both virtue and conversion to Christ are central to the life of a good society. If citizens aren't virtuous and good, good laws are of little value. They only can compel good activity externally and only then to the extent that they inspire fear. People will disobey the laws as soon as they think they can get away with it.

3. Humans are called to eternal beatitude.

This means that the highest good, the ultimate point of reference, is never civil society. There is always something more important than maintaining a healthy culture or good economy. Just as natural law supersedes civil law and society, divine law and supernatural happiness supersede civil law and natural happiness. They matter more. Someone must look out for the common good of all society, but civil society's claims can never be ultimate, nor should politics be our highest concern. Christ's kingdom is not of this world. Politics, or any human activity for that

---

[12] *Caritas in Veritate*, §26.

[13] *Centesimus Annus*, §38.

matter, cannot usher in the kingdom. That is God's doing. It is a work of grace through the Church.

The Eighth Commandment: You Shall Not Bear False Witness Against Your Neighbor

The Eighth Commandment calls us to reveal the truth in word and deed. It recognizes that truthfulness is at the heart of healthy human relationships. It also recognizes that without truthfulness, our witness to God is compromised (CCC 2464).

We know the importance of truth from our own experience. None of us want the truth hidden from us. Likewise, when someone lies to us, we feel hurt, angry, and disappointed. Truth is a necessary ingredient for all healthy relationships. It's a necessary ingredient for all healthy societies as well. Without mutual confidence in one another, there could be no society. Think of how often you have to trust that someone else is telling the truth: politicians, policemen, teachers, even the clerk at the grocery store. Society would cease to function if we could never take someone at his or her word.

Our desire for truth and our orientation toward truthfulness stems from the fact that we are made in the image of God, and God, as the Catechism reminds us, "*is the source of all truth*. His Word is truth. His Law is truth" (CCC 2465). Likewise, "in Jesus Christ, the whole of God's truth has been made manifest" (CCC 2466). Jesus described himself as the "light of the world" (John 8:12) and "the way, the truth, and the life" (14:6). He also promised "whoever believes in me may not remain in darkness" (12:46) and that "the truth will make you free" (8:32).

Living as the image of God that we are requires living in truth. Only when we are truthful can healthy relationships and cultures grow. And only by knowing the truth can we act as we should. We must know the truth about a situation, about people, about right and wrong, and about ourselves in order to make good decisions. Right action depends on right knowledge.

Given the importance of truth, it's vital that we speak it, act it, and uphold it. On the most basic level, this means we must not lie. Lying is the most direct offense against the truth. A lie is to say what is false knowing that it is false. This can be done with words, but it also can be done with actions.

When we lie with actions, this is called dissimulation (CCC 2468). It is dissimulation to present yourself in a way you are not. For example, if you go up to receive Holy Communion when you are in a state of mortal sin, in addition to committing the sin of sacrilege, you also are dissimulating. You are saying with your actions that you are not in a state of serious sin, when, in fact, you are. Hypocrisy, or publicly condemning the very sin you secretly commit, is also a kind of dissimulation, as is boasting (exaggerated bragging about one's good qualities) and irony, which is exaggerated disparaging of one's bad qualities (CCC 2481).

Other ways we can bear false witness to our neighbors is through contumely, which is dishonoring another in his or her presence. This could involve insulting someone verbally in the presence of other people or doing something to publicly humiliate someone, like refusing to let someone sit with you in the cafeteria.

It is also a sin to defame another; this is when one secretly dishonors another in speech. Defamation comes in two types: calumny and detraction (CCC 2479). We calumniate someone when we say they have a fault that they do not really have. So, if you tell someone that your friend Sara is jealous, when she's not, you're committing the sin of calumny. We commit the sin of detraction when we unjustly reveal a genuine but hidden fault. So, if you tell Nicole that Sara is selfish (which she really is), but Nicole doesn't know this about Sara, that's detraction. So many of us commit sins of defamation so often that it's easy to tell ourselves that it's not a sin or not a really serious one. St. Thomas Aquinas, however, says otherwise:

> It is a serious matter to take away the good esteem of another, because among man's temporal possessions nothing is more precious than his good name; if he lacks this he is prevented from

doing many good things . . . and therefore detraction considered in itself is grievously sinful.[14]

Yet another sin against the Eighth Commandment is the sin of rash judgment, which is choosing to believe that another person has done something wrong without actually knowing all the facts of the situation (CCC 2478).

Finally, flattery, adulation, and complaisance violate the Eighth Commandment when they "[encourage] and [confirm] another in malicious acts and perverse conduct" (CCC 2480).

Truth is fundamentally important to happiness, both now and in eternity. And yet, that does not mean we should always reveal the truth (CCC 2488–2492). If someone, for example, has asked us to keep a secret and nobody is being harmed by that secret, we owe it to that person to keep their secret. This could be a personal secret for a friend, a professional secret for our employer, or a state secret for our government. That we can only reveal a secret in case of urgent necessity (i.e. someone is being harmed by the secret) is true of all types of secrets: secrets we discover without consent (such as a hidden sin), promised secrets, as well as secrets belonging to some kind of profession. There are certain kinds of secrets, though, such as those told under the seal of Confession, can never be revealed for any reason.

There are other occasions when we can soften the truth. If a friend asks you how a dress looks on her and it looks awful, you don't have to state it quite that bluntly. A gentle, "Hmmm . . . maybe you should try another one," will do. Being brutally honest, with no thought for how our words will make someone feel, is not loving or kind.

These sins against truthfulness and justice are not only the case for our private and interpersonal lives, but are also true for media. The public has a right to information, but the demands of justice, charity, and truthfulness must all be met (CCC 2494). Civil leaders as well as journalists need these virtues too. Civil leaders must make sure the common good is served by mass media. Defamation, lies, and flattery are as sinful in

---

[14] ST II-II, q. 73, a. 2.

the media (and perhaps more so because of the potential for scandal), as they are in our individual lives. As consumers of media and users of social media, we must be conscientious not only of others' participation in these evils, so that they not derail us, but also of our complacency in them.

Lastly, it's important to note that the Catholic Church not only promotes truth in deed and word, but also in cases "beyond words" (CCC 2500). Both art and music give voice to the truth in a way beyond words. What is true and good always calls humans beyond themselves, giving glory to God. As the Catechism says:

> For this reason bishops, personally or through delegates, should see to the promotion of sacred art, old and new, in all its forms and, with the same religious care, remove from the liturgy and from places of worship everything which is not in conformity with the truth of faith and the authentic beauty of sacred art [Cf. SC 122–127]. (CCC 2503)

The Ninth Commandment: You Shall Not Covet Your Neighbor's Wife

The Ninth Commandment can sound like it's simply repeating the Sixth Commandment: no sexual sin. But it actually goes deeper than that by calling for a special respect for marriage vows, commanding the virtue of modesty, and reiterating the necessity of avoiding lust and pornography (CCC 2522).

Marriage, as we've already discussed, is both an indissoluble union and a social reality. Married persons have promised, in the presence of the community, to give themselves wholly to one another. Marriage is social by nature, not only because it necessarily involves two people, but also because it is the fundamental unit of society. The spouses themselves respect this reality by living conjugal chastity. Others live this by the chastity proper to their station in life.

To covet another's spouse, therefore, is not only a sin against chastity, but also a sin against the social aspect of marriage. The community who witnessed a couple's union is called to strengthen and support that union, not undermine it. To lust after another person's spouse damages the common good, the children of that union, and the union itself. Even more so, it damages our characters, which are shaped by the desires—good and bad—that we nurse within our hearts.

The Ninth Commandment is also fulfilled by the virtue of modesty. In some circles, the word "modesty" is used interchangeably with the word "frumpy." Mention modesty and people automatically start arguing about skirt lengths or thinking of denim jumpers and burqas. But modesty isn't a byword for bad taste. Nor is it something only women have to think about. Rather, it's the virtue that helps all of us—men and women—ensure that people see our value as a person, not just as a body.

In a fallen world, far too many of us struggle to see others as the image of God. This is particularly true when it comes to members of the opposite sex. Concupiscence makes it easy to reduce a person to their sexual value—to how attractive they are and how much pleasure looking at them and being intimate with them can give us. This isn't just true of the people we date, but also of the people we see at school, on the street, or at work. Often, a person's attractiveness is the first thing that registers with us. And when they're wearing clothes meant to emphasize their sexual desirability or when they're speaking and acting in ways meant to do the same (think of sexually suggestive conversations or dancing), it can become difficult to see anything beyond their sexual desirability. The value of the whole person—their intelligence, sense of humor, sensitivity, or caring heart—gets lost. All that is seen is the value of their body.

This is where modesty comes in. Modesty is related to the virtue of temperance, and it calls us dress, act, and talk in such a way that people can more readily see us, not just our bodies. In a sense, it asks us to moderate our desire to be sexually desirable so that other desires—like the desire to be known, loved, and appreciated for who we are—also can be fulfilled. It doesn't say we have to be frumpy or unattractive. It doesn't mandate that we never dress fashionably. It simply calls us to dress, talk, sit, dance, and act in such a way that everything that makes us attractive—not just our breasts or our biceps—can be seen.

As such, modesty aids all people in living and seeking purity of heart.

Those who are pure in heart "have attuned their intellects and wills to the demands of God's holiness, chiefly in these areas: charity [Cf. *1 Tim* 4:3–9; *2 Tim* 2:22]; chastity or sexual rectitude [Cf. *1 Thess* 4:7; *Col* 3:5; *Eph* 4:19]; [and] love of truth and orthodoxy of faith [Cf. *Titus* 1:15; *1 Tim* 1:3–4; *2 Tim* 2:23–26]" (CCC 2518). Modesty protects us from becoming the object of another person's covetous looks, and it protects others from being objectified by us.

As for what is and isn't modest . . . there is no specific list. The Church has long held that what is considered modest hinges, in part, upon the culture. Meaning, it will vary from person to person, time to time, place to place, and circumstance to circumstance.[15] There is no absolute standard on what is modest. But that doesn't give us a free pass on dressing and acting however we want. Each of us is called to think deeply about how we can dress and act in a modest way. We're also called to listen to others, especially those in authority like parents, teachers, and priests, about what is considered modest in our own place and time. The call to practice modesty is a call that must be heard in our hearts. We have to really want to protect ourselves and others from distorting the sexual value of the person.

One more thing should be kept in mind about modesty. Because it is a virtue, we can fail to live it by both deficiency and excess. The defect of modesty is lewdness. Lewdness is most evident in pornography, but essentially it's any exaggerated display of sexuality. On the flip side, the excess of modesty is prudishness. We fall into this vice when we are so overly careful in dress and activity that we are functionally claiming the human body is evil. Modesty is the mean between these vices: not drawing others into sin through lewdness, but also not implying that realities God created are bad.

---

[15] Aquinas, ST I-II, q. 64, a. 1.

The Tenth Commandment: You Shall Not Covet Your Neighbor's Goods.

The Tenth Commandment is the last of the Decalogue, and extends the prohibition of the Ninth Commandment to our neighbor's property. Like the Ninth Commandment, it is concerned with the sins of the heart, of the wrong feelings we nurse inside us. Unlike the Ninth Commandment, though, it's concerned with material goods, not persons.

One of the primary sins we "nurse" inside us is greed (CCC 2536). Greed is an inordinate desire for more of something than we need: this could be food, money, cars, sweaters, shoes, houses, jewelry, etc. The problem here isn't with the things themselves. Food is good. Cars are helpful. Clothes are essential. The real problem is with our desires—wanting too much of a thing or wanting something when we don't need it. For instance, going on a shopping spree when we already have enough clothing is wanting too much of something when we don't actually have a need for it. That's greed. In this case our desire for the thing is twisted, and our inability to check that twisted desire leads us to make bad choices.

Another sin we "nurse" inside our hearts is envy (CCC 2358–2340). Envy is sadness in the face of another's good. It's when we see the house or the shoes or the car somebody else has and feel sad—not because them possessing that thing hurts us or them in any way, but because we want it instead of them. Envy is the fruit of competition. We see the good as limited and our neighbors as competitors. We think because we don't have something that we want, nobody else should have it either.

In order to check our covetous desires, God calls us to instead cultivate a spirit of liberality and generosity—of giving to others without counting the cost. He also calls us to cultivate humility—to recognize that the desires of our own heart can lead us astray, to see our own faults and virtues in light of him, and to think of others more than ourselves. And he calls us to temperance, or moderation—to seek temperance in all things. The Church doesn't condemn riches or assert that being rich or poor are good things in themselves. Both must be seen in light of Christ and the choices we make in response to what we have been given. Likewise, whether rich or poor, whatever we possess must be held lightly, meaning if we lost it tomorrow, we could go on without great sadness.

At the same time, it helps to remember that less can be more. This is why religious brothers and sisters take vows of poverty. By possessing little, we are freed to dedicate ourselves to God. We are less likely to become attached to the things of this world and experience what Jesus warned us about when he said, "Truly, I say to you, it will be hard for a rich man to enter the kingdom of heaven. Again I tell you, it is easier for a camel to go through the eye of a needle than for a rich man to enter the kingdom of God" (Matt 19:23–24).

Those of us called to live in the world have to find the balance between wealth and poverty, between owning things, but not letting them (or the desire for them) own us. This balance is what Jesus means when he talks about the poor in spirit (Matt 5:3). To be poor in spirit is to possess what is necessary for the work and life God has entrusted to us, but, by God's grace, to remain detached from those goods so that we can use them for love of God and neighbor.

SELECTED READING
Benedict XVI, Encyclical Letter on Integral Development in Charity and Truth *Caritas in Veritate* (June 29, 2009), nos. 2–7

Charity is at the heart of the Church's social doctrine. Every responsibility and every commitment spelt out by that doctrine is derived from charity which, according to the teaching of Jesus, is the synthesis of the entire Law (cf. Mt 22:36–40). . . .

I am aware of the ways in which charity has been and continues to be misconstrued and emptied of meaning, with the consequent risk of being misinterpreted, detached from ethical living and, in any event, undervalued. In the social, juridical, cultural, political and economic fields—the contexts, in other words, that are most exposed to this danger—it is easily dismissed as irrelevant for interpreting and giving direction to moral responsibility. Hence the need to link charity with truth not only in the sequence, pointed out by

Saint Paul, of *veritas in caritate* (Eph 4:15), but also in the inverse and complementary sequence of *caritas in veritate*. Truth needs to be sought, found and expressed within the "economy" of charity, but charity in its turn needs to be understood, confirmed and practised in the light of truth. In this way, not only do we do a service to charity enlightened by truth, but we also help give credibility to truth, demonstrating its persuasive and authenticating power in the practical setting of social living. This is a matter of no small account today, in a social and cultural context which relativizes truth, often paying little heed to it and showing increasing reluctance to acknowledge its existence.

Through this close link with truth, charity can be recognized as an authentic expression of humanity and as an element of fundamental importance in human relations, including those of a public nature. *Only in truth does charity shine forth*, only in truth can charity be authentically lived. Truth is the light that gives meaning and value to charity. That light is both the light of reason and the light of faith, through which the intellect attains to the natural and supernatural truth of charity: it grasps its meaning as gift, acceptance, and communion. Without truth, charity degenerates into sentimentality. Love becomes an empty shell, to be filled in an arbitrary way. In a culture without truth, this is the fatal risk facing love. It falls prey to contingent subjective emotions and opinions, the word "love" is abused and distorted, to the point where it comes to mean the opposite. Truth frees charity from the constraints of an emotionalism that deprives it of relational and social content, and of a fideism that deprives it of human and universal breathing-space. In the truth, charity reflects the personal yet public dimension of faith in the God of the Bible, who is both *Agápe* and *Lógos*: Charity and Truth, Love and Word.

Because it is filled with truth, charity can be understood in the abundance of its values, it can be shared and communicated. *Truth*, in fact, is *lógos* which creates *diá-logos*, and hence communication and communion. Truth, by enabling men and women to let go of their subjective opinions and impressions, allows them to move beyond cultural and historical limitations and to come together in the assessment of the value and substance of things. Truth opens and unites our minds in the *lógos* of love: this is the Christian proclamation and testimony of charity. In the present social and cultural context, where there is a widespread tendency to relativize truth, practising charity in truth helps people to understand that adhering to the values of Christianity is not merely useful but essential for building a good society and for true integral human development. A Christianity of charity without truth would be more or less interchangeable with a pool of good sentiments, helpful for social cohesion, but of little relevance. In other words, there would no longer be any real place for God in the world. Without truth, charity is confined to a narrow field devoid of relations. It is excluded from the plans and processes of promoting human development of universal range, in dialogue between knowledge and praxis.

Charity is love received and given. It is "grace" (*cháris*). Its source is the wellspring of the Father's love for the Son, in the Holy Spirit. Love comes down to us from the Son. It is creative love, through which we have our being; it is redemptive love, through which we are recreated. Love is revealed and made present by Christ (cf. Jn 13:1) and "poured into our hearts through the Holy Spirit" (Rom 5:5). As the objects of God's love, men and women become subjects of charity, they are called to make themselves instruments of grace, so as to pour forth God's charity and to weave networks of charity.

This dynamic of charity received and given is what gives rise to the Church's social teaching, which is *caritas in veritate in re sociali:* the proclamation of the truth of Christ's love in society. This doctrine is a service to charity, but its locus is truth. Truth preserves and expresses charity's power to liberate in the ever-changing events of history. It is at the same time the truth of faith and of reason, both in the distinction and also in the convergence of those two cognitive fields. Development, social well-being, the search for a satisfactory solution to the grave socio-economic problems besetting humanity, all need this truth. What they need even more is that this truth should be loved and demonstrated. Without truth, without trust and love for what is true, there is no social conscience and responsibility, and social action ends up serving private interests and the logic of power, resulting in social fragmentation, especially in a globalized society at difficult times like the present.

"*Caritas in veritate*" is the principle around which the Church's social doctrine turns, a principle that takes on practical form in the criteria that govern moral action. I would like to consider two of these in particular, of special relevance to the commitment to development in an increasingly globalized society: *justice and the common good.*

First of all, justice. *Ubi societas, ibi ius*: every society draws up its own system of justice. *Charity goes beyond justice*, because to love is to give, to offer what is "mine" to the other; but it never lacks justice, which prompts us to give the other what is "his," what is due to him by reason of his being or his acting. I cannot "give" what is mine to the other, without first giving him what pertains to him in justice. If we love others with charity, then first of all we are just towards them. Not only is justice not extraneous to charity, not only is it not an alternative or parallel path to charity: justice is inseparable from charity, and intrinsic to it. Justice is the primary way of charity or, in Paul VI's words, "the minimum measure" of it, an integral part of the love "in deed and in truth" (1 Jn 3:18), to which Saint John exhorts us. On the one hand, charity demands justice: recognition and respect for the legitimate rights of individuals and peoples. It strives to build the *earthly city* according to law and justice. On the other hand, charity transcends justice and completes it in the logic of giving and forgiving. The *earthly city* is promoted not merely by relationships of rights and duties, but to an even greater and more fundamental extent by relationships of gratuitousness, mercy and communion. Charity always manifests God's love in human relationships as well, it gives theological and salvific value to all commitment for justice in the world.

Another important consideration is the common good. To love someone is to desire that person's good and to take effective steps to secure it. Besides the good of the individual, there is a good that is linked to living in society: the common good. It is the good of "all of us," made up of individuals, families and intermediate groups who together constitute society. It is a good that is sought not for its own sake, but for the people who belong to the social community and who can only really and effectively pursue their good within it. To desire the *common good* and strive towards it *is a requirement of justice and charity*. To take a stand for the common good is on the one hand to be solicitous for, and on the other hand to avail oneself of, that complex of institutions that give structure to the life of society, juridically, civilly, politically and culturally, making it the *pólis*, or "city." The more we strive to secure a common good corresponding to the real needs of our neighbours, the more effectively we love them. Every Christian is called to practise this charity, in a manner corresponding to his vocation and according to the degree of influence he wields in the *pólis*. This is the institutional path—we might also call it the political path—of charity, no less excellent and effective than the kind of charity which encounters the neighbour directly, outside the institutional mediation of the *pólis*. When animated by charity, commitment to the common good has greater worth than a merely secular and political stand would have. Like all commitment to justice, it has a place within the testimony of divine charity that paves the way for eternity through temporal action. Man's earthly activity, when inspired and sustained by charity, contributes to the building of the universal *city of God*, which is the goal of the history of the human family. In an increasingly globalized society, the common good and the effort to obtain it cannot fail to assume the dimensions of the whole human family, that is to say, the community of peoples and nations, in such a way as to shape the *earthly city* in unity and peace, rendering it to some degree an anticipation and a prefiguration of the undivided *city of God*.

QUESTIONS FOR REVIEW

1. What is the "universal destination of goods"?
2. What are three theological foundations of Catholic Social Thought?
3. Why is lying wrong? What are four other ways you can break the Eighth Commandment besides lying?
4. What is the virtue of modesty and how does it help us honor the Ninth Commandment?
5. What are greed and envy and how do they lead to people violating the Tenth Commandment?

QUESTIONS FOR DISCUSSION

1. The Seventh Commandment calls us to value people more than wealth. What consequences do you see in our world from people failing to do this?
2. What are some of the ways you've seen people violate the Eighth Commandment on social media? Why is it so easy to break this commandment?
3. Where do you find your value as a person? How can the virtue of modesty help you protect yourself from being valued in the wrong way?

PART III

GOD'S GUIDANCE:

THE LAWS OF THE NEW COVENANT

In God's plan for our salvation, the Old Law and the New Law—the Old Covenant and New Covenant, Old Testament and New Testament— weren't separate plans. God didn't try one plan, and when that didn't work out, try another. Rather his plan, known as the economy of salvation, was one plan . . . with two parts.

The Old Covenant was the first part of God's plan. Jesus' coming began the second part. Because of the unity of God's plan, Jesus doesn't abolish all the laws that had come before him. Rather, as he explains, "Do not think that I have come to abolish the law and the prophets; I have come not to abolish them but to fulfil them" (Matt 5:17). Likewise, throughout his earthly ministry, Jesus recommends the Ten Commandments multiple times, both explicitly (e.g. Matt 19:16–22), and implicitly (e.g. Matt 22:35–40).

Jesus does more than simply fulfill and endorse the Ten Commandments, though; he perfects them. He does this by calling us to live them interiorly, as well as exteriorly, asking us to let the commandments shape our characters, as well as our acts. To make that possible, he also supplies us with the grace we need to keep the commandments, making us able to live the law in a way that wasn't possible before his coming.

Chapter 1

The Two Greatest Commandments

We can better understand what Jesus did if we look at a conversation he has in the Gospel of Matthew. There, a great scholar of the law approaches Jesus to test him. He asks, "which is the great commandment in the law?" (Matt 22:36). Jesus answers him, "You shall love the Lord your God with all your heart, and with all your soul, and with all your mind. This is the great and first commandment" (22:37–38).

With this answer, Jesus summarizes the first three commandments perfectly. If we love God, we will not have other gods before him. If we love God, we will honor him and not take his name in vain. If we love God, we will keep holy the Sabbath day. In short, Jesus makes love the animating principle by which we keep the commandments. The commandments shouldn't be kept out of fear. Rather, they should be kept out of a true love for God. But Jesus isn't done with his answer. He continues: "And a second is like it, You shall love your neighbor as yourself" (Matt 22:39).

The second great commandment relates to commandments four through ten. Jesus fulfills them by making love the animating principle by which we relate to our neighbors, as well as God. We honor our parents out of love. We no longer avoid murder for fear of punishment, but rather out of love for our neighbor. We live the gift of our sexuality in truth out of love for ourselves and our neighbor. We don't steal out of love for our neighbor. We don't lie out of love for our neighbor. We don't covet—persons or things—out of love for our neighbor. Love becomes the reason for everything we do . . . and don't do.

By giving us these two great commandments, Jesus brings the law to completion and fullness. Love, however, is a difficult thing to command. How can Jesus command love?

The answer is that Jesus does more than issue commands; he also gives us the grace we need to obey his commands. God never commands the impossible, and through the grace of the Holy Spirit, we're able to live not just the letter of the law, but also the spirit of the law, allowing it to transform our hearts so that it actually becomes a joy to obey God's commands. For this reason, St. Thomas Aquinas wrote that the heart of the New Covenant is the grace of the Holy Spirit given to the faithful through the virtue of faith and working through charity.[1]

SELECTED READING
John Paul II, General Audience, October 6, 1999[2]

The Apostle John urges us: "Beloved, let us love one another; for love is of God, and he who loves is born of God and knows God. He who does not love does not know God; for God is love" (1 Jn 4:7–8).

While these sublime words reveal to us the very essence of God as a mystery of infinite charity, they also lay the basis for the Christian moral life, which is summed up in the commandment of love.

The human person is called to love God with total commitment and to relate to his brothers and sisters with a loving attitude inspired by God's own love. Conversion means being converted to love.

In the Old Testament the inner dynamics of this commandment can already be seen in the covenant relationship established by God with Israel: on the one hand, there is the initiative of God's love, and, on the other, the response of love that he expects from Israel. This

---

[1] Aquinas, ST I-II, q. 106, a. 1.
[2] Available online at https://w2.vatican.va/content/john-paul-ii/en/audiences/1999/documents/hf_jp-ii_aud_06101999.html

is how, for example, the divine initiative is presented in the Book of Deuteronomy: "It was not because you were more in number than any other people that the Lord set his love upon you and chose you, for you were the fewest of all peoples; but it is because the Lord loves you" (Dt 7:7–8). The basic commandment that directs Israel's entire religious life corresponds to this preferential, totally gratuitous love: "You shall love the Lord your God with all your heart, and with all your soul, and with all your might" (ibid., 6:5).

The loving God is a God who is not remote, but intervenes in history. When he reveals his name to Moses, he does so to assure him of his loving assistance in the saving event of the Exodus, an assistance which will last for ever (cf. Ex 3:15). Through the prophets' words, he would continually remind his people of this act of love. We read, for example, in Jeremiah: "Thus says the Lord: 'The people who survived the sword found grace in the wilderness; when Israel sought for rest, the Lord appeared to him from afar. I have loved you with an everlasting love; therefore I have continued my faithfulness to you'" (Jer 31:2–3).

It is a love which takes on tones of immense tenderness (cf. Hos 11:8f.; Jer 31:20) and normally uses the image of a father, but sometimes is also expressed in a spousal metaphor: "I will betroth you to me for ever; I will betroth you to me in righteousness and in justice, in steadfast love and in mercy" (Hos 2:19; cf. vv. 18–25).

Even after seeing his people's repeated unfaithfulness to the covenant, this God is still willing to offer his love, creating in man a new heart that enables him to accept the law he is given without reserve, as we read in the prophet Jeremiah: "I will put my law within them, and I will write it upon their hearts" (Jer 31:33). Likewise in Ezekiel we read: "A new heart I will give you, and a new spirit I will put within you; and I will take out of your flesh the heart of stone and give you a heart of flesh" (Ez 36:26).

In the New Testament this dynamic of love is centered on Jesus, the Father's beloved Son (cf. Jn 3:35; 5:20; 10:17), who reveals himself through him. Men and women share in this love by knowing the Son, that is, by accepting his teaching and his work of redemption.

We can only come to the Father's love by imitating the Son in his keeping of the Father's commandments: "As the Father has loved me, so have I loved you; abide in my love. If you keep my commandments, you will abide in my love, just as I have kept my Father's commandments and abide in his love" (ibid., 15:9–10). In this way we also come to share in the Son's knowledge of the Father: "No longer do I call you servants, for the servant does not know what his master is doing; but I have called you friends, for all that I have heard from my Father I have made known to you" (ibid., v. 15).

Love enables us to enter fully into the filial life of Jesus, making us sons in the Son: "See what love the Father has given us, that we should be called children of God; and so we are. The reason why the world does not know us is that it did not know him" (1 Jn 3:1). Love transforms life and enlightens our knowledge of God to the point that it reaches that perfect knowledge of which St Paul speaks: "Now I know in part; then I shall understand fully, even as I have been fully understood" (1 Cor 13:12).

It is necessary to stress the relationship between knowledge and love. The inner conversion which Christianity offers is a genuine experience of God, in the sense indicated by Jesus in his priestly prayer at the Last Supper: "This is eternal life, that they know you the only true God, and Jesus Christ whom you have sent" (Jn 17:3). Knowledge of God, of course, also has an intellectual dimension (cf. Rom 1:19–20), but the living experience of the Father and the Son occurs through love, that is, in the last analysis, in the Holy Spirit, because "God's love has been poured into our hearts through the Holy Spirit" (Rom 5:5).

The Paraclete is the One through whom we experience God's fatherly love. Moreover, the most comforting effect of his presence in us is precisely the certainty that this eternal and boundless love with which God loved us first will never abandon us: "Who shall separate us from the love of Christ? . . . For I am sure that neither death, nor life, nor angels, nor principalities, nor things present, nor things to come, nor powers, nor height, nor depth, nor anything else in all creation, will be able to separate us from the love of God in

Christ Jesus our Lord" (ibid., 8:35, 38–39). The new heart, which loves and knows, beats in harmony with God who loves with an everlasting love.

QUESTIONS FOR REVIEW

1. What is the greatest commandment?
2. What is the second greatest commandment?
3. How does the greatest commandment fulfill the first three of the Ten Commandments?
4. How does the second greatest commandment fulfill the last seven of the Ten Commandments?
5. What is the heart of the new covenant?

QUESTIONS FOR DISCUSSION

1. What do you think it looks like to love God with your whole heart, mind, soul, and strength? What is one practical way you could show your love for God more each day?
2. What are some of the ways you show love for yourself each day?
3. What do you think it looks like to love your neighbor as yourself? What is one practical way you could show your love for others more each day?

Chapter 2

The Sermon on the Mount

As we've already discussed, because of our fallen human nature, it often can feel like God's law is interfering with our happiness by getting in the way of what we want. In reality, though, God's law isn't interfering with our happiness at all. It's simply interfering with *our wrong ideas* of what will make us happy. We're the problem; not the law. The law is a good thing. The whole reason it exist is to help us live in accord with our nature and find the fulfillment we want to find.

Again, though, God's ideas of what will make us happy often run contrary to the world's ideas of what will make us happy. The world promises us we will be happy if we have more stuff: more power, more wealth, more fame, more sex, more things. During Jesus' earthly ministry he turned the world's idea of happiness on its head. He did this especially in one of his most famous sermons, the Sermon on the Mount.

The Beatitudes

|| ASSIGNED READING
|| Matthew 5:1–11

Teaching atop a large hill, with thousands of people listening, Jesus outlined the secret to happiness, to blessedness, to beatitude. There are eight "beatitudes" in total in that sermon—eight things Jesus said we must do and be to experience ultimate happiness.

Let's look at each a little more closely, to see what these beatitudes mean for us.

1. Blessed Are the Poor in Spirit, for Theirs Is the Kingdom of Heaven.

Traditionally, to be poor in spirit means to be humble. It means to see ourselves as God sees us—no better, no worse—recognizing that we are fallen creatures in need of God's grace, and dependent on him for every breath we take and every good thing we do.

When we see ourselves this way, God becomes the priority. We seek him in all things and find our consolation in him. The more we recognize that he is the source of true happiness, the more true happiness we find, and the more we start experiencing the joy that the saints experience in heaven.

Jesus is the perfect example of being poor in spirit since he is perfectly humble (lowly) and not attached to the things of this world. "Take my yoke upon you, and learn from me; for I am gentle and lowly in heart, and you will find rest for your souls. For my yoke is easy, and my burden is light" (Matt 11:29).

2. Blessed Are Those Who Mourn, for They Shall Be Comforted.

For all who've experienced grief, this beatitude can, at first glance, not ring true. After all, deep sadness can last for years; comfort doesn't automatically come. But according to St. Gregory of Nyssa, Jesus isn't talking about ordinary mourning. Rather, he's talking about the type of mourning that leads us closer to God, such as mourning over our sins or mourning over the conditions of this world.[1]

Feeling sorry for the wrong we've done is one of the most important steps we must take on our journey to heaven. If we don't feel sorry for the wrong we've done—if we don't mourn over sin and feel regret not just for getting caught, but also for hurting ourselves, hurting others, and going against God—then we can't receive the comforts of heaven in this life or the next. Nor can we begin taking the necessary steps to change our ways.

---

[1] Gregory of Nyssa, *Gregory of Nyssa: Homilies on the Beatitudes*, ed. Hubertus Drobner and Albert Viciano (Leiden: Brill, 2000), III:2 (40).

That's why sadness over sin, known as "contrition," is one of the prerequisites for receiving absolution in confession.

Jesus is the perfect example of this virtue, not because he repented of his own sin (he had none), but because the virtue of contrition also extends to mourning over others' sins and the situation of this world. "And when he drew near and saw the city he wept over it, saying, 'Would that even today you knew the things that make for peace! But now they are hidden from your eyes'" (Luke 19:41–42).

3. Blessed Are the Meek, for They Shall Inherit the Earth.

When people think of meekness in the modern world, they often think of someone who is submissive or a pushover—someone who never speaks their mind and lets others walk all over them. This, however, is not what Jesus is recommending. He's instead speaking of the virtue of meekness in the traditional sense, which is self-possession in the face of adversity. More simply put, meekness is the virtue that helps us to control our anger and express it in the correct ways. It helps us to not fly off the handle and say the first thing that pops into our heads.

This doesn't mean we should be passive in the face of evil. Rather, it means we shouldn't respond to evil with evil; meekness ensures that we don't. Anger drives God out of our souls; meekness invites him in.

Jesus, as with all the beatitudes, is the ultimate example of this. When Jesus got angry—and he did get angry, condemning the corrupt Pharisees as "whitewashed tombs" (Matt 23:27) and driving the money changers out of the temple (21:12–17)—he never lost control. He was zealous for the good, but able to direct his anger at the right targets, in the right ways, and to the right degree.

4. Blessed Are Those Who Hunger and Thirst for Righteousness, for They Shall Be Satisfied.

When we hunger and thirst for righteousness, we hunger and thirst for right order. We desire justice. We desire our actions to be perfectly in line with the good, the true, and the beautiful. We also desire everyone else's actions to be in line with the good, the true, and the beautiful as well. We want to see everyone—including our friends, family, teachers, employers, and perfect strangers—doing God's will and doing it consistently, promptly, and joyfully.

This right order, of course, is made possible only by God's grace and can be found fully only in heaven. But those who hunger for righteousness now are, to some extent, able to begin taking part in heaven here. We're able to feel the satisfaction that comes from being in God's will and doing what we were made to do. Then, when we get to heaven, the satisfaction we feels goes even deeper, because we're in perfect communion with God and all his saints. Our entire existence in heaven is marked by righteousness, by right order.

As with the above beatitudes, Jesus is the perfect example of this. He is, after all, called "the righteous" one (1 John 2:1).

5. Blessed Are the Merciful, for They Shall Obtain Mercy.

Mercy is both a feeling and an action. St. Thomas Aquinas defined it as "the compassion in our hearts for another person's misery, a compassion which drives us to do what we can to help him."[2] The *feeling* of mercy is compassion (also known as "affective" mercy), which means looking at another person who is suffering—who is poor, hungry, grieving, sick, lonely, or lost—and feeling sorrow for their sorrow. The *action* of mercy is doing "what we can to help him" (also known as "effective" mercy), which means taking direct steps to alleviate the person's sorrow—giving them money, clothes, food, drink, medicine, company, or whatever else they need.

When we are merciful, when we feel compassion and act on what we feel, we image God, who showers us daily with his merciful love. We also draw closer to God, becoming more united to him in love as we share his mercy with others. And, as Jesus says here, we receive God's mercy as we show his mercy, for when we show mercy to others, God shows even more mercy to us.

When we look to Jesus, we see him showing us how to be merciful. Not only do we see him feeding, healing, and comforting people, but, ultimately, we see him on the Cross, having so much compassion on us and wanting so badly to deliver us from our sins that he gives his life for us. "For you know the grace of our Lord Jesus Christ, that though he was rich, yet for your sake he became poor, so that by his poverty you might become rich" (2 Cor 8:9).

---

[2] Aquinas, ST II-II, q. 30, a. 1.

6. **Blessed Are the Pure in Heart, for They Shall See God.**

When our bodies are unclean, there are things we can't (or shouldn't) do. For example, we can't go into nice restaurants covered in mud. We can't attend important meetings stinking of sweat. If the Queen of England or the pope wanted to meet with us, we would take a shower, brush our hair, and put on clean clothes before we went.

God, who is infinitely more important than the Queen of England, wants a similar cleanliness from us when we appear before him in heaven. The only difference is, God wants our souls to be clean. He wants us to be free from the spiritual grime that laziness, lies, lust, anger, greed, envy, pride, and selfishness cake onto our soul. He doesn't expect us to clean our souls on our own, though. In large part, he does it for us, giving us the grace we need to come to him in the Sacrament of Penance, confess our sins, and begin a new life.

With enough time and enough grace, this helps us live in the light of God's love in this world. And someday, it will help us to look upon God as he is in heaven, and know him as Jesus, who is all pure, knows him (1 John 3:3).

7. **Blessed Are the Peacemakers, for They Will Be Called Sons of God.**

When nations stop waging war upon each other, we say they are at peace. But peace is so much more than just the cessation of fighting. Peace is the rest caused by right order between all things and God. Right order precludes conflict. It doesn't allow for fighting or unrest or even unease. It is perfect rest, perfect contentment in God's goodness and love.

We can experience this rest as individuals, feeling it in our own hearts. We also can experience it in our relationships with others—united to one another in love and understanding and trust, because we are united to God. Peacemakers are those who work to bring this rest about, who work to help people love and understand each other, who strive to build bridges and increase respect for human dignity among all people. As we do this, we image Jesus, who himself became a bridge between man and God, so that humanity could be reconciled to Our Father in heaven.

8. **Blessed Are Those Who Are Persecuted for Righteousness' Sake, for Theirs Is the Kingdom of Heaven.**

If you choose to always do the right thing, if you choose to follow God's ways and not the world's ways, one thing is inevitable: persecution. In one way or another, people will make it difficult for you to do good. They might tease you or mock you. They might refuse to be your friend or date you. They even might deny you your job, good reputation, freedom, or life.

As for why people do this . . . all sorts of reasons exist: some people feel judged by others' good choices and don't want to change their own behavior; other people worry God will get in the way of their friendship with us, don't want to see us be truly happy, or simply don't know or understand truth and goodness.

Regardless of why people persecute us for doing what's right, when it happens, we mustn't be surprised. Jesus promised us exactly this. "Remember the word that I said to you," he told his Apostles. "'A servant is not greater than his master.' If they persecuted me, they will persecute you" (John 15:20).

This, however, is exactly why we are "blessed" when we're persecuted for righteousness' sake: because in our suffering, we are united to Jesus, who suffered the ultimate persecution on the Cross. Just like with the other beatitudes, in enduring persecution for Jesus' sake, we become more like Jesus. We image more perfectly "him whom they have pierced" (John 19:37).

Jesus' Other Teachings

The remainder of the Sermon on the Mount includes several other teachings that are essential to the New Law in the New Covenant.

1. "Love Your Enemies and Pray for Those Who Persecute You."

ASSIGNED READING
Matthew 5:43–48

It's part of the natural law to love those who love us and care for those who care for us. Reason dictates that we do that, which is why, during the time of the Old Covenant, both Israel and people of other nations recognized the wisdom of loving your neighbor. For them, that meant their immediate family and friends. You loved your tribe. You stayed close to your tribe. You cared for your tribe. Such love, people realized, was necessary for survival.

At the same time, the ancient Israelites and nearly all others agreed that the people you didn't love were your enemies. Love for those who hate you, who want to hurt you, who don't want you to be happy, made no sense to them. After all, loving people who hate you isn't necessary for physical survival. In fact, if all you're worried about is keeping your body alive, loving your enemies may be the last thing you want to do. But Jesus is concerned about more than our bodies. He's concerned about our souls. And our souls, in order to live eternally, must be governed by love for everyone—friends and enemies alike.

When Jesus calls us to love our enemies and pray for those who persecute us, he is perfecting the natural law and elevating it; he's giving us a higher law—a supernatural law, or a divine law. This divine law calls us to love as God loves: without distinction. God loves sinners and saints alike. He has loved us into existence, and he continues to hold us in his love every minute of our life. We exist because God wants us to exist. In us, he sees his image. So, Jesus tells us, we must do the same. We must see every human being—no matter who they are or what they've done—as the image of God. We must see God in them, and we must love them for that.

This is what Jesus did throughout his life, including on the Cross. As St. Paul says:

> While we were yet helpless, at the right time Christ died for the ungodly. Why, one will hardly die for a righteous man—though

perhaps for a good man one will dare even to die. But God shows his love for us in that while we were yet sinners Christ died for us. (Rom 5:6–8)

As disciples, we abide in this love and are called to share it with others. "This is my commandment, that you love one another as I have loved you" (John 15:12).

2. "Do Not Be Anxious About Tomorrow."

ASSIGNED READING
Matthew 6:25–34

If you had to sum up Matthew 6:25–34, you could do it in one word: trust. Trust is what Jesus calls us to here. He calls us to trust in God's love, trust in God's care, and trust in God's goodness. He's not saying we shouldn't work for the necessities of life, expecting food to magically appear on our table and clothes to magically appear in our closets. What he *is* saying is that we need to keep our priorities straight and not panic.

By asking, "Is not life more than food, and the body more than clothing?" (Matt 6:25) Jesus reminds us that food is for life and clothing for the body. It's not the other way around. The way we spend our time and energy should reflect that. On a different level, our lives and everything we possess exist for the sake of our relationship to the kingdom. They're supposed to help us and others grow closer to the Lord. This is why it's not wrong to seek the goods of this world, but it is wrong to seek them in a way that is not conducive to holiness.

As we seek these things, we need to always remember that God is Father: he knows what we truly need. We're not to panic when things don't go as we expect them to go. The kingdom is what really matters, and other things only matter in relation to it.

3.   *"Do Not Resist One Who Is Evil."*

|| ASSIGNED READING
|| Matthew 5:38–39

Some interpret this passage to claim that Jesus recommends complete nonresistance. So, they would argue, if someone raised a gun to shoot you, you should let them. More people, though, including the Catholic Church, interpret this passage to mean that we should resist evil and injustice, but not use evil means to do so. We should not seek revenge or be unjust in our anger. According to this interpretation, a better translation would be "do not seek vengeance against the evildoer." Instead, we are called to overcome evil with good (Rom 12:19–2).

Moreover, according to this interpretation, since violence is not the topic of the passage, you may resist the evildoer violently, if necessary. So, if someone jumps you on the street, in the dark, you can hit them; if another country's army invades your country, your country's army can mobilize and fight back. In neither example are you seeking revenge. You are not attacking the other because he attacked you. Rather, you are preventing them, with violence if necessary, from completing the evil they set out to do.

4.   *"Judge Not."*

|| ASSIGNED READING
|| Matthew 7:1–3

"Judge not" is a favorite saying in our culture. When someone is told they're doing something wrong, it's an easy retort. "Who are you to judge me?" they'll ask. "Who are you to judge what I am doing is wrong? 'Judge, not,' said the Lord."

But Jesus wasn't telling the crowds that they were never allowed to judge the moral rightness or wrongness of actions. We're supposed to judge the moral rightness and wrongness of actions. That's why God gave us the Ten Commandments, and the two greatest commandments, and the Beatitudes, and all the other teachings in the Gospels and the Epistles: so that we can judge right from wrong, so that we know what we should be doing in order to be truly happy. Discernment of the good, in every situation, using the wisdom of revelation, is the business of every Christian.

What's *not* the business of every Christian is judging souls. We may know that a person is doing something objectively wrong. We may know they have lied, discriminated, murdered, stolen, cheated, fornicated, and done any number of bad things, and we can know with certainty that those things, those actions, are bad. What we can't know is why a person did something, how much freedom they exercised, or how much knowledge of the good they have. We can't judge intentions, and we can't judge whether a soul is on its way to heaven or on its way to hell. That is a judgment left to God alone. To even condemn a person's intentions is rash judgment—a sin prohibited by the Eighth Commandment.

After telling us that we can't judge anyone's soul, Jesus advises that we focus instead on something we can control: our own sinful behaviors. Oftentimes, focusing on others' sins is just a good excuse to avoid dealing with our own sins. And we all have plenty of those. Nobody but Jesus and the Blessed Mother has been born without sin, and each of us falls short in some way (usually lots of ways) of the example set for us by Jesus. Working on rooting out the plank in our own eye, and thinking less about the splinter in another's, is Jesus' way of telling us to attend to our own sins, lest we become the hypocrites that the Pharisees were, cruelly judging others while doing nothing to correct ourselves.

SELECTED READING
St. Thomas à Kempis, *The Imitation of Christ*, chaps. 1–2

The First Chapter: Imitating Christ and Despising All Vanities on Earth

"He who follows Me, walks not in darkness," says the Lord. By these words of Christ we are advised to imitate His life and habits, if we wish to be truly enlightened and free from all blindness of heart. Let our chief effort, therefore, be to study the life of Jesus Christ.

The teaching of Christ is more excellent than all the advice of the saints, and he who has His spirit will find in it a hidden manna. Now, there are many who hear the Gospel often but care little for it because they have not the spirit of Christ. Yet whoever wishes to understand fully the words of Christ must try to pattern his whole life on that of Christ.

What good does it do to speak learnedly about the Trinity if, lacking humility, you displease the Trinity? Indeed it is not learning that makes a man holy and just, but a virtuous life makes him pleasing to God. I would rather feel contrition than know how to define it. For what would it profit us to know the whole Bible by heart and the principles of all the philosophers if we live without grace and the love of God? Vanity of vanities and all is vanity, except to love God and serve Him alone.

This is the greatest wisdom—to seek the kingdom of heaven through contempt of the world. It is vanity, therefore, to seek and trust in riches that perish. It is vanity also to court honor and to be puffed up with pride. It is vanity to follow the lusts of the body and to desire things for which severe punishment later must come. It is vanity to wish for long life and to care little about a well-spent life. It is vanity to be concerned with the present only and not to make provision for things to come. It is vanity to love what passes quickly and not to look ahead where eternal joy abides.

Often recall the proverb: "The eye is not satisfied with seeing nor the ear filled with hearing." Try, moreover, to turn your heart from the love of things visible and bring yourself to things invisible. For they who follow their own evil passions stain their consciences and lose the grace of God.

The Second Chapter: Having a Humble Opinion of Self

Every man naturally desires knowledge; but what good is knowledge without fear of God? Indeed a humble rustic who serves God is better than a proud intellectual who neglects his soul to study the course of the stars. He who knows himself well becomes mean in his own eyes and is not happy when praised by men.

If I knew all things in the world and had not charity, what would it profit me before God Who will judge me by my deeds?

Shun too great a desire for knowledge, for in it there is much fretting and delusion. Intellectuals like to appear learned and to be called wise. Yet there are many things the knowledge of which does little or no good to the soul, and he who concerns himself about other things than those which lead to salvation is very unwise.

Many words do not satisfy the soul; but a good life eases the mind and a clean conscience inspires great trust in God.

The more you know and the better you understand, the more severely will you be judged, unless your life is also the more holy. Do not be proud, therefore, because of your learning or skill. Rather, fear because of the talent given you. If you think you know many things and understand them well enough, realize at the same time that there is much you do not know. Hence, do not affect wisdom, but admit your ignorance. Why prefer yourself to anyone else when many are more learned, more cultured than you?

If you wish to learn and appreciate something worthwhile, then love to be unknown and considered as nothing. Truly to know and despise self is the best and most perfect counsel. To think of oneself as nothing, and always to think well and highly of others is the best and most perfect wisdom. Wherefore, if you see another sin openly or commit a serious crime, do not consider yourself better, for you do not know how long you can remain in good estate. All men are frail, but you must admit that none is more frail than yourself.

QUESTIONS FOR REVIEW

1. What are the eight beatitudes and what is the meaning of each?
2. How does Jesus call us to treat our enemies and how does he give us an example of this?
3. What attitude toward God does Jesus call us to cultivate when he tells us not to be anxious about tomorrow?

4. How does the Church understand Jesus' teaching, "Do not resist one who is evil"?

5. What does Jesus mean when he tells us, "Judge not"?

QUESTIONS FOR DISCUSSION

1. Of all the eight beatitudes, which is the easiest for you to identify with? Which is the most difficult to identify with? Explain.

2. Do you struggle with anxiety? If so, why do you think this is? How could greater trust in God and his plan help you with this?

3. Why do you think so many people want to apply Jesus' command to "judge not" to actions, and not just souls?

Chapter 3

The Law and Jesus' Church

When it comes to God's laws, it's easy to see why we need to obey the Ten Commandments: God himself wrote them in stone. It's also easy to see why we need to obey the commands Jesus gave in the Gospels. He's the Son of God, so if he says something, it's probably wise to obey.

But what about the Church's laws? What about no meat on Fridays during Lent? What about excommunication for desecrating the Eucharist? What about requiring Mass attendance every Sunday? Do we really need to obey them? What authority do a bunch of men in Rome, living and dead, have over us?

Answering those questions begins by looking at what (or who) the Church is.

The Nature of the Church

Assigned Reading
Matthew 16:3–20

At first glance, the Church can feel like something of a third wheel. There's you, and there's Jesus—what more do you need? Why should you care what the Church has to say?

The simplest answer to that question is, "Because Jesus says so." While he was still on earth, Jesus announced to St. Peter that he had plans for him:

> And I tell you, you are Peter, and on this rock I will build my
> Church, and the gates of Hades shall not prevail against it. (Matt
> 16:18)

Later, before he ascended into heaven, Jesus entrusted his eleven
remaining Apostles with an authority that he entrusted to no one else:
the power to forgive sins.

> If you forgive the sins of any, they are forgiven; if you retain the
> sins of any, they are retained. (John 20:23)

He also charged them with baptizing people "in the name of the
Father and of the Son and of the Holy Spirit" (Matt 28:18) and offering
the Eucharist "in remembrance of me" (Luke 22:19).

The Apostles understood from the first that Jesus had entrusted his
kingly and priestly authority to them (Acts 6:6). Jesus knew his followers
needed community, as well as a hierarchy of leaders to serve those followers, so he established the Church.

The Apostles also understood that it was their job to pass that authority on to others—to successors—who could continue preaching, teaching, and celebrating the sacraments after they were gone. In turn, those
successors knew it was their job to pass that authority down to successors
of their own. And so it has continued to the present day, with the Apostles'
successors—the pope and bishops—carrying on the work first entrusted
by Jesus to Peter and the Apostles: the leadership, governance, and care of
the Church:

> You then, my son, be strong in the grace that is in Christ Jesus, and
> what you have heard from me before many witnesses entrust to
> faithful men who will be able to teach others also. (2 Tim 2:1–2)

The Magisterium

Taken collectively in their teaching authority received from Jesus, the pope and the bishops in union with him are called the "magisterium." The magisterium has three fundamental purposes.

The most fundamental purpose of the magisterium is to proclaim the revelation of Jesus Christ (CCC 85–87). It is through the Church's magisterium that the Good News of Jesus Christ reaches all generations. The magisterium's second purpose is to define those beliefs and actions that are incompatible with the faith—that are contrary to God's saving love and a life of eternal friendship with him. The magisterium's third purpose is to clarify revelation and explain it, so that each new generation can understand Jesus' teaching and hear his call.

In all these ways, the magisterium preserves what Jesus taught so that we can have true faith. Without it, his revelation of himself would have been lost or corrupted. This applies not only to the work of copying, translating, and safeguarding Sacred Scripture, but also to preserving and handing on Sacred Tradition.

Sacred Scripture is the Word of God. It is an essential part of God's revelation of himself. But Scripture itself isn't enough. Scripture never tells us which books count as Scripture, how to interpret Scripture, or how to derive any conclusions from Scripture. Only Sacred Tradition, handed on through a living teaching authority, can do that.

Two thousand years ago, shortly after Jesus' Ascension into heaven, an Ethiopian eunuch discovered this very truth when he traveled to Jerusalem and began studying the Jewish scriptures. The Book of Acts recounts:

> [The Apostle] Philip ran to him, and heard him reading Isaiah the prophet, and asked, "Do you understand what you are reading?" And [the Ethiopian] said, "How can I, unless some one guides me?" And he invited Philip to come up and sit with him. . . . And the eunuch said to Philip, "Please, about whom does the prophet say this, about himself or about some one else?" Then Philip opened his mouth, and beginning with this Scripture he told him the good news of Jesus. (Acts 8:30–31, 34–35)

Today, the Catholic magisterium continues Philip's (and all the Apostles') work, guiding the world in its understanding of the Good News

THE LAW AND JESUS' CHURCH

of Jesus. The magisterium teaches the faith, refutes errors, and explains beliefs. This is true regarding both questions of faith—dogma such as the Trinity, the Incarnation, and the sacraments—and morals.

Not surprisingly, some people object to this. They don't mind the Church making proclamations about the Immaculate Conception and the Trinity, but when it comes to morals—with whom they sleep, how they treat their family, or how they spend their money—they argue that it's none of the Church's business. Jesus thinks otherwise. Through his Incarnation, death, and Resurrection, he revealed the way to true happiness. He then entrusted the task of handing on what he revealed to his Church. It is the Church's job to hand that on in turn, both proclaiming definitively what Jesus revealed about happiness and what is incompatible with Jesus' message.

The Charism of Infallibility

The bishops don't do this proclaiming, refuting, and explaining on their own. Their teaching and judgments aren't simply a matter of their own personal opinions. Rather, "In order to preserve the Church in the purity of the faith handed on by the apostles, Christ who is the Truth willed to confer on her a share in his own infallibility" (CCC 889).

The charism of infallibility guarantees that the pope and the bishops speaking in union with him (the magisterium) will not teach any error on any questions concerning faith and morals. The Holy Spirit protects them, when they teach definitively and officially, from teaching something that is untrue regarding the deposit of faith. So, this means they won't say that God is two Persons or that marriage is anything other than the union of one man and one woman. They can't. The Holy Spirit won't permit it.

There are limits to this special charism. First, it only applies to faith and morals—not to questions of science or sports or culture. A pope's opinion on the health benefits of the Paleo diet or who will win the World Cup is just that: an opinion. Likewise, even on questions of faith and morals, the charism of infallibility only guarantees that the pope and the bishops in union with him won't say the wrong thing; it doesn't guarantee that they will say everything that needs to be said or say it in the very best way possible. Finally, it only applies in certain circumstances. Popes and bishops, in private conversations, speeches, and interviews, can and have made errors. Infallibility is a charism exercised only in three specific circumstances and with one important condition: the pope—or the bishops together with the pope—must proclaim something as definitively belonging to revelation or definitively incompatible with revelation (CCC 891).

1. The pope can make such a proclamation on his own when he explicitly states that he is speaking *ex cathedra*, which means "from his chair" (the pope's chair or throne is the symbol of the full power of the papal office). *Ex cathedra* proclamations are known as "extraordinary" exercises of the charism of infallibility and are very rare.

2. The pope and bishops can also teach explicitly together in an ecumenical council, known as the "extraordinary universal magisterium." Like *ex cathedra* statements, extraordinary pronouncements of the universal magisterium are rare in the history of the Church.

3. Last and most common, the bishops, united throughout the world, can all proclaim something to be central to faith and morals. This is known as the "ordinary magisterium" and whenever one bishop is teaching what the Church has always taught, he is exercising the authority of the ordinary magisterium.

Even when the charism of infallibility is not being exercised, though, the bishops are still our spiritual fathers, the successors of the Apostles, who are guided by the Holy Spirit in their teaching. This means we owe them faithful assent, and entails respectfully listening to them, trusting them, and giving their judgments the weight that both their office and the circumstances merit. The Fathers of the Second Vatican Council explained:

For bishops are preachers of the faith, who lead new disciples to Christ, and they are authentic teachers, that is, teachers endowed with the authority of Christ, who preach to the people committed to them the faith they must believe and put into practice, and by the light of the Holy Spirit illustrate that faith. They bring forth from the treasury of Revelation new things and old, making it bear fruit and vigilantly warding off any errors that threaten their flock. Bishops, teaching in communion with the Roman Pontiff, are to be respected by all as witnesses to divine and Catholic truth. In matters of faith and morals, the bishops speak in the name of Christ and the faithful are to accept their teaching and adhere to it with a religious assent.[1]

In short, those who seek true happiness ought to look to the Church as they look to Jesus. She is truly both *mater et magistra*—mother and teacher—and to her teachings Jesus calls us to respond with the same response he asks us to give to him: a response of love.

Canon Law

The very mission of Jesus and the Holy Spirit are continued in and through the Church. Thus, the Church's guidance regarding the moral life is not an addition to Jesus' and the Spirit's guidance; rather, it is an application of their guidance. The Church gives us this guidance through her law, which is called "canon law."

The glossary of the Catechism of the Catholic Church defines canon law as:

The rules (canons or laws) which provide the norms for good order in the visible society of the Church. Those canon laws that apply universally are contained in the Codes of Canon Law. The most recent Code of Canon Law was promulgated in 1983 for the Latin (Western) Church and in 1991 for the Eastern Church (The Code of Canons of the Eastern Churches).

---

[1] *Lumen Gentium*, §25.

Canon law holds a similar place in the Church that civil law holds in society. That is, it has a similar relation to the New Law that civil law has to natural law. Much of what is in canon law simply *repeats* what is in the New Law; it just applies it to concrete situations. For example, Jesus made clear the necessity of fasting (Matt 6:16–18); canon law makes sure we fast by giving us specific days to do that. Other canon laws are *derived* from the New Law; they make explicit what the New Law implied. They do this either by "conclusion" or "determination."

An example of a law by conclusion is the canon law that prohibits desecration of the Eucharist. We know already that the New Law prohibits sacrilege (1 Cor 11:27), which forbids the mistreatment of the sacred. Since there is nothing more sacred than the Eucharist, which is Jesus' Body and Blood, the Church *concludes* that it is a sacrilege to desecrate the Eucharist.

An case of a law by determination is the law regarding how often Catholics must receive the Eucharist. The New Law makes it clear that one must receive the Eucharist (John 6:53; 1 Cor 11:23–26), but nowhere does it state how often that must happen. The Church thus *determines* that one must receive the Eucharist at least once a year (CCC 2042).

Another example of a law of determination is the Eucharistic fast. Revelation makes it clear that we must prepare ourselves to receive the Eucharist in the New Law (1 Cor 11:28), but it does not say what form this preparation should take. The Church makes the determination we must have no food one hour prior to receiving the Eucharist.

The important distinction between a determination and a conclusion is that determinations can be changed by the proper authority. Conclusions cannot change. So, it is and always will be a sacrilege to desecrate the Eucharist, but if the Church wants to change the length of time we need to fast before receiving the Eucharist, it can (and has).

Some canon laws are both conclusions and determinations. The Precepts of the Church fall into this category. These precepts outline the necessary minimums of spiritual and moral effort for Catholics. The New Law requires all of these, but does not say how often. The Church both concludes that these things must be done and determines how often we must do them in order to consider ourselves practicing Catholics. These precepts are:

1. Honor Sunday and holy days of obligation by Mass attendance;
2. Make a good confession once a year;
3. Receive the Eucharist at least during the Easter season;
4. Observe the days of fasting and abstinence;
5. Provide for the material needs of the Church.

Of course, these precepts only apply to people who can actually fulfill those obligations. A prisoner of war who can't get to Mass isn't guilty of disobeying a precept of the Church. A gravely ill person who can't fast isn't guilty of anything, either. For the rest of us, though, those are the bare minimum requirements for remaining in good standing with the Church. They are part of the Church's guidance based on the New Law. This is not an external imposition on believers' freedom, but a help given to us by the Church so that we can live the lives for which we were made.

Of course, the Church's authority is not limited to the conclusions and determinations of the New Law. Her authority extends to the natural law as well. Remember, sins against the natural law are also sins against the New Law. Jesus never abolished the Old Law; he fulfilled it and perfected it. Because of her divine authority, the Church can see the dictates of the natural law and understand those dictates more clearly than any other earthly authority. The Church truly understands what it means for all people to obey the natural law.

Accordingly, the Church must speak on issues of natural law—on sex and marriage, just wages and labor rights, crime and punishment. To keep silent on these issues would negate her very mission of leading people to happiness in Christ. That is something she cannot do.

SELECTED READING
Second Vatican Council, Dogmatic Constitution on the Church *Lumen Gentium* (November 21, 1964), nos. 18–21

For the nurturing and constant growth of the People of God, Christ the Lord instituted in His Church a variety of ministries, which work for the good of the whole body. For those ministers, who are endowed with sacred power, serve their brethren, so that all who are of the People of God, and therefore enjoy a true Christian dignity, working toward a common goal freely and in an orderly way, may arrive at salvation.

This Sacred Council, following closely in the footsteps of the First Vatican Council, with that Council teaches and declares that Jesus Christ, the eternal Shepherd, established His holy Church, having sent forth the apostles as He Himself had been sent by the Father; and He willed that their successors, namely the bishops, should be shepherds in His Church even to the consummation of the world. And in order that the episcopate itself might be one and undivided, He placed Blessed Peter over the other apostles, and instituted in him a permanent and visible source and foundation of unity of faith and communion. And all this teaching about the institution, the perpetuity, the meaning and reason for the sacred primacy of the Roman Pontiff and of his infallible magisterium, this Sacred Council again proposes to be firmly believed by all the faithful. Continuing in that same undertaking, this Council is resolved to declare and proclaim before all men the doctrine concerning bishops, the successors of the apostles, who together with the successor of Peter, the Vicar of Christ, the visible Head of the whole Church, govern the house of the living God.

The Lord Jesus, after praying to the Father, calling to Himself those whom He desired, appointed twelve to be with Him, and whom He would send to preach the Kingdom of God; and these apostles He formed after the manner of a college or a stable group, over which He placed Peter chosen from among them. He sent them first to the children of Israel and then to all nations, so that as sharers in His power they might make all peoples His disciples, and sanctify and govern them, and thus spread His Church, and by ministering to it under the guidance of the Lord, direct it all days even to the consummation of the world. And in this mission they were fully confirmed on the day of Pentecost in accordance with the Lord's promise: "You shall receive power when the Holy Spirit comes upon you, and you shall be witnesses for me in Jerusalem, and in all Judea and in Samaria, and even to the very ends of the earth." And the apostles, by preaching the Gospel everywhere, and it being accepted by their hearers under the influence of the Holy Spirit, gather together the universal Church, which the Lord established on the apostles and built upon blessed Peter, their chief, Christ Jesus Himself being the supreme cornerstone.

That divine mission, entrusted by Christ to the apostles, will last until the end of the world, since the Gospel they are to teach is for all time the source of all life for the Church. And for this reason the apostles, appointed as rulers in this society, took care to appoint successors.

For they not only had helpers in their ministry, but also, in order that the mission assigned to them might continue after their death, they passed on to their immediate cooperators, as it were, in the form of a testament, the duty of confirming and finishing the work begun by themselves, recommending to them that they attend to the whole flock in which the Holy Spirit placed them to shepherd the Church of God. They therefore appointed such men, and gave them the order that, when they should have died, other approved men would take up their ministry. Among those various ministries which, according to tradition, were exercised in the Church from the earliest times, the chief place belongs to the office of those who, appointed to the episcopate, by a succession running from the beginning, are passers-on of the apostolic seed. Thus, as St. Irenaeus testifies, through those who were appointed bishops by the apostles, and through their successors down in our own time, the apostolic tradition is manifested and preserved.

Bishops, therefore, with their helpers, the priests and deacons, have taken up the service of the community, presiding in place of God over the flock, whose shepherds they are, as teachers for doctrine, priests for sacred worship, and ministers for governing. And just as the office granted individually to Peter, the first among the apostles, is permanent and is to be transmitted to his successors, so also the apostles' office of nurturing the Church is permanent, and is to be exercised without interruption by the sacred order of bishops.

Therefore, the Sacred Council teaches that bishops by divine institution have succeeded to the place of the apostles, as shepherds of the Church, and he who hears them, hears Christ, and he who rejects them, rejects Christ and Him who sent Christ.

In the bishops, therefore, for whom priests are assistants, Our Lord Jesus Christ, the Supreme High Priest, is present in the midst of those who believe. For sitting at the right hand of God the Father, He is not absent from the gathering of His high priests, but above all through their excellent service He is preaching the word of God to all nations, and constantly administering the sacraments of faith to those who believe, by their paternal functioning. He incorporates new members in His Body by a heavenly regeneration, and finally by their wisdom and prudence He directs and guides the People of the New Testament in their pilgrimage toward eternal happiness. These pastors, chosen to shepherd the Lord's flock of the elect, are servants of Christ and stewards of the mysteries of God, to whom has been assigned the bearing of witness to the Gospel of the grace of God, and the ministration of the Spirit and of justice in glory.

For the discharging of such great duties, the apostles were enriched by Christ with a special outpouring of the Holy Spirit coming upon them, and they passed on this spiritual gift to their helpers by the imposition of hands, and it has been transmitted down to us in Episcopal consecration. And the Sacred Council teaches that by Episcopal consecration the fullness of the sacrament of Orders is conferred, that fullness of power, namely, which both in the Church's liturgical practice and in the language of the Fathers of the Church is called the high priesthood, the supreme power of the sacred ministry. But Episcopal consecration, together with the office of sanctifying, also confers the office of teaching and of governing, which, however, of its very nature, can be exercised only in hierarchical communion with the head and the members of the college. For from the tradition, which is expressed especially in liturgical rites and in the practice of both the Church of the East and of the West, it is clear that, by means of the imposition of hands and the words of consecration, the grace of the Holy Spirit is so conferred, and the sacred character so impressed, that bishops in an eminent and visible way sustain the roles of Christ Himself as Teacher, Shepherd and High Priest, and that they act in His person. Therefore it pertains to the bishops to admit newly elected members into the Episcopal body by means of the sacrament of Orders.

QUESTIONS FOR REVIEW

1. What is the magisterium and what authority does it have?
2. What does the charism of infallibility guarantee?
3. Under what circumstances is the charism of infallibility exercised?
4. What is canon law and what does it do?
5. What is the difference between a canon law made by conclusion and a canon law made by determination?

QUESTIONS FOR DISCUSSION

1. What value do you see in Jesus establishing a hierarchy with the ability to teach and make determinations about the moral law? Do you think this is important and helpful? Why or why not?
2. What is the danger of not recognizing the Holy Spirit's role in guiding the magisterium?
3. How seriously do you take the "small" laws of the Church, like fasting before Holy Communion and practicing some voluntary penance on Friday? Explain.

PART IV

THE REALITY OF SIN AND GRACE:

LIVING OUR NEW LIFE IN CHRIST JESUS

Chapter 1

THE REALITY OF SIN

The reality of sin is obvious. We see it all around us in broken homes and broken lives. People choose again and again what is not good for them. Not only do they suffer for that, but so do all the people around them. For this, in part, we have our first parents to thank. Adultery, murder, lust, greed—all stem from original sin, from the privation of grace we have inherited from Adam and Eve.

But Adam and Eve don't get all the blame. There is also actual sin, sin committed by us due to the enduring effects of concupiscence. We all, in some form or other, commit the same sins as Adam and Eve. We all do what is wrong.

Sin isn't all the same, though. There are different types of sin and different levels of gravity. To break any of the laws we've talked about in the last two parts of this book is sinful, but how sinful depends upon the sin and upon us—upon our knowledge and our freedom.

Two Categories of Sin

The two main categories of sin are "mortal" and "venial." Venial sins strain our relationship with others and God. If God's life were like a light in our soul, venial sins would dim that light. They wouldn't make it go dark; they don't kill the life of God in us. But they do wound that life or inhibit it. They make the light that should burn bright, burn less light. Moreover, the more venial sins we commit without repenting, the dimmer the light grows. Small sins increasingly make it difficult for us to see the difference between right and wrong, so stealing little things frequently can lead to stealing big things. Telling little lies can lead to telling big lies. Committing small sins of lust can lead to committing big sins of lust. Venial sin, while not deadly, is always dangerous.

Mortal sin, on the other hand, is always deadly. The word mortal comes from the Latin word *mors*, which literally means death. Mortal sin is a deadly sin, a sin that snuffs out the life of sanctifying grace in our soul. They are actions incompatible with a living relationship with God and incompatible with love of God and neighbor. Three factors must be present to commit a mortal sin: full knowledge, full consent, and grave matter.

Full knowledge means we must know the action is wrong. Trying to tell ourselves something isn't wrong means we know it's wrong. Likewise, suspecting something is wrong and choosing not to find out for certain is what the Church calls "willful ignorance," and that doesn't get us off the hook either. Neither does refusing to listen to people who try to tell us something is wrong. All those scenarios still count as "full knowledge." In fact, they make the sin even worse, explains the Catechism: "Feigned ignorance and hardness of heart [Cf. Mk 3:5–6; Lk 16:19–31] do not diminish, but rather increase, the voluntary character of a sin" (CCC 1859).

Second, we must fully consent to the action for it to be a mortal sin. We have to really *choose* to sin, with full freedom and without any form of coercion. Violence and the threat of violence, emotions, bio-physiological conditions, or social conditions all can limit our freedom. So, if someone forces your hand to pull a trigger and kill someone, you didn't sin. That is violent coercion. Likewise, certain passions also can limit freedom, such as fear or anger. Sometimes, we say or do wrong things in the heat of the moment, without fully thinking them through or without even realizing what we are doing. This doesn't mean the actions aren't still wrong; they are. But they might only be venially sinful, not mortally sinful. Then again, if we knew we were putting ourselves in a situation where emotions might lead us to do something sinful, that increases our culpability and consent. Finally, certain bio-physiological and social conditions can limit our freedom. Addictions, culture, and disabilities all can inhibit freedom to the extent that we do grave actions without sinning mortally.

Finally, the action chosen freely must be grave. The action must be serious enough that by choosing it we turn ourselves away from God, rejecting both him and the order of goodness he created. Those actions directly contrary to love of God or neighbor are an example of grave actions. Violating any of the Ten Commandments and committing any one of the seven deadly sins (which we'll get to shortly) are examples of grave matter.

If all three factors are present—full knowledge, full consent, and grave matter—then the action is a rejection of God and destroys friendship with him. The life of sanctifying grace and all it causes (which we'll talk more about below) is eradicated from the soul. Happily for us, though, sin never has the last word and there is always the possibility of forgiveness in the Sacrament of Confession.

Sins, whether mortal or venial, can be committed by commission or omission. So, for example, we can commit murder by shooting someone (commission) or by not saving him (omission). We are guilty of sins of omission when we should have made an act of virtue but did not.

The Seven Deadly Sins

Whether we're sinning by omission or commission, most sins find their root in in one of the seven deadly, or "capital" sins. These sins are called capital because they give rise to the other sins in our lives. The capital sins are:

1. Pride
2. Avarice
3. Envy
4. Wrath
5. Lust
6. Gluttony
7. Sloth

Pride is the root of all sin. It is, according to St. Augustine, to put oneself in place of God.[1] Instead of viewing reality as revolving around God, the proud man sees himself as the center of the universe, the judge of all. In a sense, all sins are expressive of pride, the will to determine what is good and evil for ourselves.

Avarice, or greed, is the inordinate desire or attachment to material goods. It's wanting too much money, too much power, too much fame, and too many things. It leads to other sins when we allow those wants to control us and sin against people in our efforts to get what we want.

Envy is sadness in the face of another's good. It leads us to delight in another's misfortune and sets the stage for us actually inflicting misfortune upon others.

Wrath, or hatred, wishes evil for people directly. Sins of violence and cruelty, including murder, revenge, and torture, are just a few of the many sins rooted in wrath.

Lust is the inordinate desire for sexual pleasure. It is the beginning of all sins against the gift of sexuality—adultery, fornication, masturbation, contraception, pornography, homosexual acts, and more—because it reduces people to objects and makes pleasure the point of sexual intimacy.

Gluttony is the inordinate attachment to eating and drinking. It's not just eating too much, but also eating when we're not hungry; eating greedily, without thought for others; eating too sumptuously (always and only eating the "best" foods); and eating only foods we like and that are prepared in certain ways (i.e. being "picky").[2] Gluttony makes a god of our stomach, and leads us to sin against charity.

Finally, sloth is spiritual laziness. It is a lack of joy in the spiritual life and lack of fervor in seeking spiritual goods. When we cease to seek God fervently and take joy in him, the seeds are sown for every other kind of sin.

Capital sins are not necessarily mortal sins. They do constitute grave matter, but free consent and full knowledge must also be present in order for them to completely kill the life of God in the soul. Nevertheless, they

---

[1] St. Augustine, *Confessions* 2.6.

[2] Aquinas, ST II-II, q. 148.

are always serious, and they are always destructive. Like all sins, they are the great enemy of holiness, virtue, and happiness. Part of the Catholic tradition identifies some sins as so serious that they "cry out to heaven" (CCC 1867; cf. Gen 4:10). And as St. Paul says:

> Now the works of the flesh are plain: immorality, impurity, licentiousness, idolatry, sorcery, enmity, strife, jealousy, anger, selfishness, dissension, party spirit, envy, drunkenness, carousing, and the like. I warn you, as I warned you before, that those who do such things shall not inherit the kingdom of God. (Gal 5:19–21)

When we choose to do good and follow God's plan for beatitude, our life on earth becomes a foretaste of heaven. When we choose to sin and reject God's plan for our happiness, our life on earth becomes a foretaste of hell. As the legendary twentieth-century Christian apologist, C.S. Lewis, explained in his book *the Great Divorce*:

> [People] say of some temporal suffering, "No future bliss can make up for it," not knowing that Heaven, once attained, will work backwards and turn even that agony into a glory. And of some sinful pleasure they say, "Let me have but this and I'll take the consequences": little dreaming how damnation will spread back and back into their past and contaminate the pleasure of the sin. Both processes begin even before death. The good man's past begins to change so that his forgiven sins and remembered sorrows take on the quality of Heaven: the bad man's past already conforms to his badness and is filled only with dreariness. And that is why . . . the Blessed will say, "We have never lived anywhere except in Heaven," and the Lost, "We were always in hell." And both will speak truly.[3]

---

[3]   C.S. Lewis, *The Great Divorce*, in *The Complete C.S. Lewis Signature Classics* (New York: Harper One), 503.

Fortunately for us, help in making a heaven out of our earth comes to us in many forms.

God's Love And Mercy Through Jesus Christ

When we sin, we break the law given to us by God and, in the process, we break ourselves. That's really what sin does. Our choosing to go against God's will doesn't change his will. It doesn't make his law any less true or good. It just hurts us. It leads—sooner or later—to our unhappiness. It leads us away from God and along a path of sorrow, confusion, and ultimately, loneliness.

That is what hell is. Hell is the ultimate loneliness. It's rejecting God and casting ourselves out of the love, light, and communion that we experience in relationship with him. There is no love in hell. There is no friendship in hell. There is no happiness, no laughter, no joy. There can't be. Apart from God, those things don't exist.

Fortunately for us, God doesn't want sin to be the last word on our lives. He doesn't want anyone to spend an eternity apart from him. He doesn't even want anyone to spend an hour apart from him. So, he has moved heaven and earth to help us avoid sin and choose life.

God's Loving Plan

After Adam and Eve fell from grace in the Garden, God set in motion a plan to heal wounded humanity. He formed a family, the Israelites, called them out from the other nations, and began teaching them to walk in his ways. He also prepared them, through the prophets, for a Savior, so they would know how to recognize this Savior when he came.

Then, God himself came as that Savior. In the Incarnation, the Second Person of the Trinity took on flesh and assumed a human nature. The eternal, infinite, omnipotent, omniscient Son of God limited himself and his powers within the confines of time, space, and a human body.

Nothing short of infinite love could motivate such an act (John 3:16).

The Incarnation and all that followed—from Jesus' public ministry to his Crucifixion, death, Resurrection, and Ascension—was one great act of mercy, born out of an equally great love. Mercy, you'll recall, is love working to alleviate that which causes another pain or suffering. That's what God did for us. His love for us didn't diminish in the face of sin. Instead, it willed an even greater good for us (Rom 5:20). Jesus Christ is this greater good. He is a sign of God's continuing love and mercy for sinful humans.

Rather than let us face eternal suffering, Jesus, who is love and mercy incarnate, was sent to help us understand our fallen human condition and give us the means to transcend it, to rise above it. Jesus' coming perfected the law, revealing its true heart to us. But it did so much more. It also made it possible for us to imitate him and live in accordance with the law—in accordance with the very thing that can bring us happiness. Even more importantly, it offered us the opportunity to become more than God's creatures; it offered us the opportunity to become God's children, to put on Christ in Baptism, receive the Holy Spirit, and live a life fueled by sanctifying grace, by God's own life. It opened up the gates not just to natural happiness, but to supernatural happiness.

In this life, we are never alone. God is always there, always offering us the help we need to avoid sin and walk closely with him. It may not be easy to avoid sin, given our own fallen human natures, but with God's help, it is possible. And there is so much help available for the asking, starting with help found in grace and the virtues.

SELECTED READING
St. Augustine, *Confessions* II, chap. 2

But what was it that I delighted in save to love and to be beloved? But I held it not in moderation, mind to mind, the bright path of friendship, but out of the dark concupiscence of the flesh and the effervescence of youth exhalations came forth which obscured and overcast my heart, so that I was unable to discern pure affection from unholy desire. Both boiled confusedly within me, and dragged away my unstable youth into the rough places of unchaste desires, and plunged me into a gulf of infamy. Your anger had overshadowed me, and I knew it not. I was become deaf by the rattling of the chains of my mortality, the punishment for my soul's pride; and I wandered farther from You, and You *"suffered"* (Matthew 17:17) me; and I was tossed to and fro, and wasted, and poured out, and boiled over in my fornications, and You held Your peace, O Thou my tardy joy! Thou then held Your peace, and I wandered still farther from You, into more and more barren seed-plots of sorrows, with proud dejection and restless lassitude.

Oh for one to have regulated my disorder, and turned to my profit the fleeting beauties of the things around me, and fixed a bound to their sweetness, so that the tides of my youth might have spent themselves upon the conjugal shore, if so be they could not be tranquillized and satisfied within the object of a family, as Your law appoints, O Lord, — who thus formest the offspring of our death, being able also with a tender hand to blunt the thorns which were excluded from Your paradise! For Your omnipotency is not far from us even when we are far from You, else in truth ought I more vigilantly to have given heed to the voice from the clouds: *"Nevertheless, such shall have trouble in the flesh, but I spare you"*; (1 Corinthians 7:28) and, *"It is good for a man not to touch a woman"* (Corinthians 7:1) and, *"He that is unmarried cares for the things that belong to the Lord, how he may please the Lord; but he that is married cares for the things that are of the world, how he may please his wife"* (1 Corinthians 7:32–33). I should, therefore, have listened more attentively to these words, and, being severed *"for the kingdom of heaven's sake,"* (Matthew 19:12), I would with greater happiness have expected Your embraces.

But I, poor fool, seethed as does the sea, and, forsaking You, followed the violent course of my own stream, and exceeded all Your limitations; nor did I escape Your scourges (Isaiah 10:26). For what mortal can do so? But You were always by me, mercifully angry, and dashing with the bitterest vexations all my illicit pleasures, in order that I might seek pleasures free from vexation. But where I could meet with such except in You, O Lord, I could not find — except in You, who teachest by sorrow, (Deuteronomy 32:39) and woundest us to heal us, and killest us that we may not die from You. "Formest trouble in or as a precept." Thou makest to us a precept out of trouble, so that trouble itself shall be a precept to us, *i.e.* hast willed so to discipline and instruct those Thy sons, that they should not be without fear, lest they should love something else, and forget Thee, their true good. Where was I, and how far was I exiled from the delights of Your house, in that sixteenth year of the age of my flesh, when the madness of lust—to the which human shameless-ness grants full freedom, although forbidden by Your laws—held complete sway over me, and I resigned myself entirely to it? Those about me meanwhile took no care to save me from ruin by marriage, their sole care being that I should learn to make a powerful speech, and become a persuasive orator.

QUESTIONS FOR REVIEW

1. What is venial sin, and how does it affect our relationship with Jesus?
2. What is mortal sin and how does it affect our relationship with Jesus?
3. What conditions have to be present for a sin to be considered mortal?
4. Name and define the seven deadly sins. Why are they called "deadly"?
5. What was God's response to our sin?

QUESTIONS FOR DISCUSSION

1. Can you think of a time where a small sin you committed led to other sins? Describe what happened and how it affected your attitude towards God.
2. How have you seen sin make people "stupid"?
3. How does our culture glorify any of the seven deadly sins? How does it depict these sins? Why is this dangerous?

Chapter 2

GRACE AND THE VIRTUES

The Nature of Grace

The Biblical word for grace is the Greek *charis*, which can be translated as kindness, favor, gift, or good will. In the Christian context, grace is an expression of God's love. It is divine favor. The *Catholic Biblical Dictionary* defines grace as:

> The supernatural gift that God bestows entirely of his own benevolence upon men and women for their eternal salvation. Justification comes through grace, and through the free gift of grace the ability is bestowed to respond to the divine call of adoptive sonship, participation in the divine nature, and eternal life. Grace is more than the gifts of nature; it is a supernatural gift surpassing the attributes of created nature.[1]

God's love and favor, not surprisingly, are different from human love and favor. Our love is a reaction, or a response, to the goodness of the object we love. We love autumn because it's beautiful. We love coffee because it keeps us awake. We love bacon because it's completely delicious. Our love for those things, however, doesn't change them. Fall and

---

[1] *The Catholic Bible Dictionary*, ed. Scott Hahn (New York: Doubleday, 2009), s.v. "grace."

coffee and bacon don't get more wonderful because we love them. They are just as good before our love as after it.

God's love, on the other hand, is not reactive, but active. That is, God's love is not a response to goodness; it's the cause of goodness. God loves golden autumn leaves, but those autumn leaves are loveable only because God loves them. God loves apples, but apples only exist to be loved because God loves them. In creation, God's love causes things to be, sustains them in being, and gives them their goodness.[2]

What's true for objects is also true for subjects, for people. First, God doesn't love us because we are good. We are good because God loves us—because, like those apples, he brought us into existence and sustains our existence. Moreover, supernaturally, when God loves us in a new way, that is, gives grace, we are changed. We are renewed, restored, and redeemed. We become better—more ourselves—because of his love.

Importantly, since grace is an expression of God's love, it cannot be earned. By a totally undeserved gift, we are drawn into God's life. This is often expressed in the language of adoption (Eph 1:5). Christians are adopted sons and daughters of God, given a share of his life from one who has it naturally: Jesus. By being redeemed on the pattern of Christ, Christians are brought into relation with the Holy Trinity (Rom 8:15).

Types of Grace

This adoption occurs in the Sacrament of Baptism. In Baptism, God sets an indelible mark on our soul; he claims our soul for his own. This claim comes with a gift: sanctifying grace, which restores the gift of divine life lost by Adam and Eve and gradually heals us of the effects of that loss. As long as the soul consents to its presence, sanctifying grace abides in us habitually. Habitual sanctifying grace marks an abiding change to our nature. It raises it to supernatural life and friendship with God, inclines us to live an upright supernatural life in accord with God's call to holiness, and allows us to cooperate with God so that we can strive for holiness.

---

[2] Aquinas, ST I, q. 20, a. 2.

Another type of grace is actual grace, which is God's continual movement and guidance for our lives. It is by actual grace that God leads and prepares the soul for redemption—for the reception of sanctifying grace in Baptism. So, the preparation for grace is itself a work of grace. The promptings that lead us to hear about God, seek to learn more about God, and decide to follow God are all actual graces. Actual grace precedes sanctifying grace. It also follows it, because after receiving sanctifying grace in Baptism, God continually moves us by actual grace, prompting us to acts of virtue and making it possible for us to become cooperators in our own redemption.

Along with the grace necessary for redemption (sanctifying grace) and guidance in the use of that grace (actual grace), we also receive special graces for the building up of the Church. The special graces are called gratuitous graces or charisms (1 Cor 12). These gifts do not sanctify us like habitual and actual grace do. Rather, God gives them to us for the sanctification of others. They exist to build up the Church. The ability to teach the faith well is one example of a charism. Healing is another.

Grace and Merit

With all these different kinds of graces, God's initiative always comes first, making it possible for us to exercise true freedom—to freely choose the good.[3] And because of this grace we can actively cooperate in our own redemption.[4]

This is the foundation for the doctrine of merit. As St. Thomas Aquinas explains in the *Summa Theologica*, human activity, enlivened by grace, really does attain eternal life. It really does earn that reward. Each true act of charity, or any virtue commanded by charity, endures for eternity. Certainly no one can earn the first grace or a restoration of grace after mortal sin, but that doesn't mean one cannot merit eternal life, the first

---

[3] *Veritatis Splendor*, §22–24.
[4] Aquinas, ST I, q. 105, a. 5.

grace for another, or the continual graces necessary for sanctification.[5]

Again, without question, God makes it possible for us to freely choose the good. We owe the grace to do that to him. Yet, ultimately, each of us bears responsibility for what path we take in life and where we will spend our eternity. God compels no one to heaven, just as he compels no one to hell. All, by grace, is freely chosen (CCC 2002, 2009).

The Virtues

If grace is the light in our souls that keeps us spiritually alive, the virtues are our spiritual muscles, which help us to do all that grace prompts us to do and all that the law tells us to do. Virtue is the means by which God's law is written on the heart. It conforms our characters and desires to the law so that its commands become second nature.

The Catechism defines virtue as a "habitual and firm disposition to do the good" (CCC 1833). That is to say, it's a habit of doing the right thing—of honoring God, telling the truth, giving generously, and carrying out all sorts of other good behaviors. Virtues, i.e. good habits, perfect our human nature and contribute to authentic happiness. Vices, on the other hand, are bad habits, which contradict our human nature and detract from our happiness. Once we have a virtue or a vice, it inclines us to continue acting in that way. That's because when presented with a certain situation, unless we actively reflect and go against our inclinations, we will act out of our habits.

Habits also change our vision of the world. As St. Thomas Aquinas said, "such as a man is, such does the end seem to him."[6] Put simply, our virtues and vices change the way we see the world and how we judge things. For example, to the chaste person, abstinence seems reasonable. To the lustful person, abstinence seems unreasonable. To the generous person, liberality seems reasonable. To the greedy person, liberality seems unreasonable.

---

[5] Aquinas, ST I-II, q. 114.

[6] Aquinas, ST I-II, q. 58, a. 5.

The fact that virtue changes our vision of the world brings up three important points for growing in virtue. First, unless we have a virtue, we can't really trust our own judgment about that activity. Someone who shoplifts regularly might not be the best expert to consult on the morality of stealing. Someone who is sleeping around probably doesn't have much wisdom to offer on the value of chastity. If we're going to grow in any virtue, we need humility to recognize that our own vices often get in the way of us seeing the value of that virtue.

Second, in order to grow in a virtue, we need to know someone who excels at that virtue. We need an exemplar—someone who has modeled that virtue well in the nitty-gritty moments of everyday life.

Third, if we're particularly prone to a certain vice, to overcome that vice, we need to aim at the other extreme in order to land at the mean of virtue. So, if we are greedy, we should give away more than what seems reasonable to us, since we know our vision of what is reasonable is distorted by our greed. Those repeated acts of what seems like unreasonable giving will slowly build up the virtue, or break down the contrary inclination to vice.

The Human Virtues

When it comes to actual virtues, the Catechism breaks up virtue into two different categories: the human virtues and the theological virtues.

Human virtues are acquired primarily through our own effort. We strive to do something good, and the more often we do it, the easier it gets. So, by telling the truth, we acquire the virtue of honesty. By giving to the poor, we acquire the virtue of generosity. By avoiding pornography and other sexual sins, we acquire the virtue of chastity. In some ways, the human virtues are like any skill—painting, cooking, scoring soccer goals; the more we practice them, the easier it gets. It takes time, it takes effort, but eventually, practice makes perfect . . . or almost perfect.

That's not to say we don't need God's grace to cultivate the human virtues. We do. Moreover, in Baptism and the other sacraments, God's grace perfects these human virtues. Nevertheless, our own effort—our repeated attempts to do the good—is the main way we develop these virtues. Which is why you don't have to be Catholic or even a baptized Christian to practice the human virtues. Atheists can be honest. Pagans can be generous. Faith in Christ doesn't make practicing the human virtues possible; it just makes practicing the human virtues easier.

Of all the different human virtues (chastity, modesty, honesty, generosity, kindness, etc.), the Church identifies four as "cardinal," meaning they are the most fundamental. All the human virtues are, in some way, related to them. They are the foundation for all the other human virtues. The four cardinal virtues are: justice, prudence, temperance, and fortitude.

Prudence, explains the Catechism, is "the virtue that disposes practical reason to discern our true good in every circumstance and to choose the right means of achieving it"; it is "'right reason in action'" (CCC 1806). Or, more simply put, prudence is knowing how to do and achieve the good. Because of this, prudence guides the other virtues. In fact, it's often called the charioteer of the virtues. That is to say, because of prudence we can recognize the importance of justice, the necessity of temperance, and the value of fortitude. Because of prudence, we also can recognize the specific situations that call for justice, temperance, and fortitude, as well as all the other virtues.

Justice is "the moral virtue that consists in the constant and firm will to give their due to God and neighbor" (CCC 1807). It makes it possible for us to do the good we're supposed to do. This is true when it comes to our relationship with God, to whom we owe obedience, reverence, love, honor, and worship. It's true when it comes to our fellow man, whose dignity, worth, and humanity we are called to respect in all our actions.

Fortitude is "the moral virtue that ensures firmness in difficulties and constancy in the pursuit of the good" (CCC 1808). That is, it is the virtue that inclines us to pursue difficult goods and endure the hardships we face as we pursue those goods. It makes it possible for us to do the good we ought to do, even when it's difficult. Because of fortitude, we can choose the good, despite our own fears and weakness. We can say no to sin, even knowing that our no might cost us something we hold dear.

Temperance is "the moral virtue that moderates the attraction of pleasures and provides balance in the use of created goods" (CCC 1809). It helps us balance competing goods in service of the ultimate good. So, it helps us to know that exercise is good, but over exercising to the point where we injure our body is not good. It tells us that it's a good thing to eat a piece of the cake our mother made us for our birthday, but a bad thing to eat three pieces of cake in one sitting. It tells us that working and studying hard is important, but not as important as our health, our time with God, or our family. Basically, temperance helps us pursue the good in a reasonable and constructive way.

The more we grow in these cardinal virtues, the richer, fuller, and more deeply human our lives become. When we can habitually know the good, do the good—even when it's difficult—and pursue the good in a right and reasonable way, life just gets better. We avoid many of the painful consequences wrought by vice, and stop getting in the way of our own natural (and supernatural) happiness.

The Theological Virtues

While the human virtues enable us to live a more human life, the theological virtues help us to live a more divine life. They till the soil of our soul, enabling us to live as sons and daughters of God now and preparing us for the life we will one day live as his children in heaven (CCC 1813). Unlike the human virtues, however, the theological virtues are not acquired through effort. Rather, they are effects of sanctifying grace, which is ordinarily acquired through the sacraments (although sometimes, extraordinarily, outside the sacraments). Our good acts inspired by these virtues help them to grow, but they don't cause them to be.[7] That is God's gift alone.

There are three theological virtues: faith, hope, and love. These virtues are the very heart of the Christian life and the first fruits of the sanctifying grace given in Baptism. Because of these virtues, we're able to cooperate with God's grace. Like all virtues, they fundamentally change

---

[7] Aquinas, ST I-II, q. 114, a. 8.

the way we see the world, but they also fundamentally change who we are.

More specifically, faith helps us to see the world as God sees it. Faith, in the broad sense, is believing something to be true based on the word of another. If you do not *know* something in the strict sense (i.e. have experience of it or an indubitable argument) and still hold it to be true, you do so based on faith. In this sense, faith is ubiquitous and natural. We cannot know everything or verify everything on our own. Most of us, for example, have never circumnavigated the earth, but we still trust that the world is round. We know this based on faith, on what others we respect—teachers, scientists, astronauts, etc.—have told us.

The virtue of faith is like natural faith, only it's assenting to something precisely because God reveals it. It means believing all that God, through Scripture and Tradition, has told us to be true (CCC 1814). In this sense, the virtue of faith makes it possible for us to know supernatural truth.

This doesn't mean that faith is irrational, though. Having faith doesn't mean we throw reason out the window. When we have faith in God, we aren't blindly leaping into the dark, but rather seeing reality in its fullest light. Faith illuminates reason; it doesn't contradict it. It helps us see natural truths—truths we could know by reason alone—more fully and deeply. It also shows us supernatural truths, truths that we could never know by reason alone. This is why faith and reason are fundamentally compatible. Both are lights; both access the truth.

The second theological virtue, hope, is the habitual inclination to seek God as the source of ultimate happiness (CCC 1817). In fact, hope gives us our first taste of eternal happiness because it helps us to see God as the perfect good and motivates us to pursue a closer relationship with him now, in this life. Hope also helps us to keep our priorities straight, and not look for happiness in things that could pull us away from God. It teaches us to see the whole world in light of eternity, and desire heaven more than anything else. Lastly, hope keeps our eyes fixed on God's love and mercy, not our own weakness and sin, and in that, it prevents us from slipping into the sin of despair.

Charity is the theological virtue that helps us "love God above all things for his own sake, and our neighbor as ourselves for the love of

God" (CCC 1822). It is the greatest of all the theological virtues because it causes the most intimate union with God. All love, of course, causes unity with the object loved. In this friendship with God, though, we also love all others because of our love for God. God loves all people, so if we love God, we must also love all people, even our enemies. To love another person we must will what is truly good for them, and that is, ultimately, God himself.

Importantly, charity makes it possible for us not only to love God and our neighbor, but to love as God loves: lavishly, sacrificially, selflessly. When we possess the theological virtue of charity, we are able to love without counting the cost, without thinking about what we get out of it, and without a selfish agenda. Charity is a love that pulls us out of ourselves and into the very heart of God.

When faith, hope, and charity are alive in us, not only are we transformed, but so too are the human virtues. Prudence, justice, fortitude, and temperance take on a supernatural quality, enabling us to pursue spiritual goods. These are often referred to as the infused cardinal virtues. Like the theological virtues, they are gifts of grace, not something we acquire through our own effort. God infuses them into our souls, enabling us to use these virtues to pursue spiritual goods and enabling the virtues themselves to transform all aspects of our life in light of the Gospel.

Together, the natural virtues and the theological virtues help us live and love as God made us to live and love. They enrich our life on earth and prepare us for our life in heaven. What they *don't* do is make us perfect . . . at least not on their own. Just because every Christian receives faith, hope, and love at their baptism doesn't mean we won't sin. We will. Likewise, just because we grow in some natural virtues doesn't mean we won't still struggle with others. Again, we will.

To truly grow in holiness, to become the men and women God made us to be, we need supernatural help that goes beyond the theological virtues. We need the graces of the sacraments.

SELECTED READING
John Paul II, Encyclical Letter *Veritatis Splendor* (August 6, 1993), no. 22–24

The conclusion of Jesus' conversation with the rich young man is very poignant: "When the young man heard this, he went away sorrowful, for he had many possessions" (Mt 19:22). Not only the rich man but the disciples themselves are taken aback by Jesus' call to discipleship, the demands of which transcend human aspirations and abilities: "When the disciples heard this, they were greatly astounded and said, 'Then who can be saved?'" (Mt 19:25). *But the Master refers them to God's power*: "With men this is impossible, but with God all things are possible" (Mt 19:26).

In the same chapter of Matthew's Gospel (19:3–10), Jesus, interpreting the Mosaic Law on marriage, rejects the right to divorce, appealing to a "beginning" more fundamental and more authoritative than the Law of Moses: God's original plan for mankind, a plan which man after sin has no longer been able to live up to: "For your hardness of heart Moses allowed you to divorce your wives, but from the beginning it was not so" (Mt 19:8). Jesus' appeal to the "beginning" dismays the disciples, who remark: "If such is the case of a man with his wife, it is not expedient to marry" (Mt 19:10). And Jesus, referring specifically to the charism of celibacy "for the Kingdom of Heaven" (Mt 19:12), but stating a general rule, indicates the new and surprising possibility opened up to man by God's grace. "He said to them: 'Not everyone can accept this saying, but only those to whom it is given'" (Mt 19:11).

To imitate and live out the love of Christ is not possible for man by his own strength alone. He becomes *capable of this love only by virtue of a gift received*. As the Lord Jesus receives the love of his Father, so he in turn freely communicates that love to his disciples: "As the Father has loved me, so have I loved you; abide in my love" (Jn 15:9). *Christ's gift is his Spirit*, whose first "fruit" (cf. Gal 5:22) is charity: "God's love has been poured into our hearts through the Holy Spirit which has been given to us" (Rom 5:5). Saint Augustine asks: "Does love bring about the keeping of the commandments, or does the keeping of the commandments bring about love?" And he answers: "But who can doubt that love comes first? For the one who does not love has no reason for keeping the commandments."

"The law of the Spirit of life in Christ Jesus has set me free from the law of sin and death" (Rom 8:2). With these words the Apostle Paul invites us to consider in the perspective of the history of salvation, which reaches its fulfilment in Christ, *the relationship between the (Old) Law and grace* (the New Law). He recognizes the pedagogic function of the Law, which, by enabling sinful man to take stock of his own powerlessness and by stripping him of the presumption of his self-sufficiency, leads him to ask for and to receive "life in the Spirit." Only in this new life is it possible to carry out God's commandments. Indeed, it is through faith in Christ that we have been made righteous (cf. Rom 3:28): the "righteousness" which the Law demands, but is unable to give, is found by every believer to be revealed and granted by the Lord Jesus. Once again it is Saint Augustine who admirably sums up this Pauline dialectic of law and grace: "The law was given that grace might be sought; and grace was given, that the law might be fulfilled."

Love and life according to the Gospel cannot be thought of first and foremost as a kind of precept, because what they demand is beyond man's abilities. They are possible only as the result of a gift of God who heals, restores and transforms the human heart by his grace: "For the law was given through Moses; grace and truth came through Jesus Christ" (Jn 1:17). The promise of eternal life is thus linked to the gift of grace, and the gift of the Spirit which we have received is even now the "guarantee of our inheritance" (Eph 1:14).

And so we find revealed the authentic and original aspect of the commandment of love and of the perfection to which it is ordered: we are speaking of *a possibility opened up to man exclusively by grace*, by the gift of God, by his love. On the other hand, precisely the awareness of having received the gift, of possessing in Jesus Christ the love of God, generates and sustains the free response of a full love for God and the brethren, as the Apostle John insistently reminds us in his first Letter: "Beloved, let us love one another; for love is of God and knows God. He who does not love does not know God; for God is love. . . . Beloved, if God so loved us, we ought also to love one another. . . . We love, because he first loved us" (1 Jn 4:7–8, 11, 19).

This inseparable connection between the Lord's grace and human freedom, between gift and task, has been expressed in simple yet profound words by Saint Augustine in his prayer: "*Da quod iubes et iube quod vis*" (grant what you command and command what you will).

The gift does not lessen but reinforces the moral demands of love: "This is his commandment, that we should believe in the name of his Son Jesus Christ and love one another just as he has commanded us" (1 Jn 3:32). One can "abide" in love only by keeping the commandments, as Jesus states: "If you keep my commandments, you will abide in my love, just as I have kept my Father's commandments and abide in his love" (Jn 15:10).

Going to the heart of the moral message of Jesus and the preaching of the Apostles, and summing up in a remarkable way the great tradition of the Fathers of the East and West, and of Saint Augustine in particular, Saint Thomas was able to write that *the New Law is the grace of the Holy Spirit given through faith in Christ.* The external precepts also mentioned in the Gospel dispose one for this grace or produce its effects in one's life. Indeed, the New Law is not content to say what must be done, but also gives the power to "do what is true" (cf. Jn 3:21). Saint John Chrysostom likewise observed that the New Law was promulgated at the descent of the Holy Spirit from heaven on the day of Pentecost, and that the Apostles "did not come down from the mountain carrying, like Moses, tablets of stone in their hands; but they came down carrying the Holy Spirit in their hearts . . . having become by his grace a living law, a living book."

QUESTIONS FOR REVIEW

1. What is sanctifying grace?
2. What is actual grace?
3. What is a virtue?

4. What are the cardinal virtues? Name and define each.
5. What are the theological virtues? Name and define each.

QUESTIONS FOR DISCUSSION

1. What cardinal virtue is the easiest for you? What cardinal virtue is the hardest?
2. What virtue do you most admire when you encounter it in others?
3. What are some of the problems you have on your plate right now? How do you think the theological virtues can help you cope with or overcome some of these problems?

Chapter 3

THE SACRAMENTS

Of all the helps God gives us to live the life of grace, there is no help more important, more foundational, and more transformative than the Church's seven sacraments. These sacraments are the primary means by which God distributes the graces won by Jesus on the Cross. They are like food for our souls, with God continually using the sacraments to nourish us with his life and nurture his life within us.

Baptism and Confirmation

Our journey to heaven begins, in an active sense, with our baptism. Actual graces may lead someone to pursue Baptism, but it is through the Sacrament of Baptism that we become God's adopted child, and it is in Baptism that the Spirit is poured out upon us, conforming us to the image of the Son (Acts 1:5; 2 Cor 3:18). Baptism gives each of us the sanctifying grace—the very life of God—that Adam and Eve lost in the Garden. That sanctifying grace makes it possible for us to attain more than natural happiness; it also enables us to attain supernatural happiness. Likewise, it makes it possible for us to live more than a natural life; it also grants us the gift of supernatural life—a life of eternal friendship with God. For this reason, when we're baptized, we are truly born again, receiving a new life in the Spirit (John 3:5).

Because the infusion of grace received in Baptism moves us toward God—toward supernatural happiness—Baptism also moves us away from the opposite of happiness: sin. It washes us clean of any and all past sins, both original sin and all actual sin. Concupiscence, however, which is our inclination to sin, remains. This internal tension between the newly acquired supernatural virtues and the remaining inclination to sin gives Christian life its perennial character: struggle, continual conversion, and repentance.

Baptism not only purifies us from all sin but also recreates us, making us a partaker of the divine nature (2 Pet 1:4). Once baptized, we are co-heirs with Christ (Rom 8:17) and temples of the Holy Spirit (1 Cor 6:19).

Sanctifying grace causes all these things. Sanctifying grace conforms us to God, deifying us (CCC 1999). Sanctifying grace infuses the supernatural virtues and the gifts of the Holy Spirit into our soul. And sanctifying grace enables true freedom so that we can consent to the promptings of God's actual graces and cooperate with those graces, making possible our growth in spiritual maturity.

This new life of grace and virtue, first received in Baptism, is strengthened in Confirmation, where the gifts and presence of the Holy Spirit is intensified within us (Acts 19:6). With this sacrament, not only does the Holy Spirit strengthen us to struggle against sin and attain perfect happiness, but also to witness and do battle for the Gospel (CCC 1303). The increase of sanctifying grace in Confirmation makes our bond to the Church more perfect and gives us the grace necessary to live as true witnesses to Christ—living the faith in word and deed, speaking out against sin, and speaking up for Jesus and his Church in the midst of a hostile culture.

Importantly, the change wrought by Baptism and Confirmation can never be revoked. Jesus claims us and marks us indelibly, both in Baptism and in Confirmation. From the moment of our baptism on, we belong to God, and are called to live in accord with what we have received, no matter how far we subsequently stray.

Likewise, the marks given in Baptism and Confirmation not only stamp us as Christ's, but also make it possible for us to receive the other sacraments and to participate in the heart of the Church's life: the Eucharistic celebration. Functionally, these sacraments enroll us in the Body of Christ—the Catholic Church—and make us heirs to all the promises of the New Covenant. We commit to living lives of truth and love within the Church, as witnesses to Christ, while the Church commits to giving us all the help we need to do that through her sacraments and teaching.

For this reason, Baptism, Confirmation, and the Eucharist are collectively known as the sacraments of initiation (CCC 1229). Through these sacraments unity with Jesus and the Church is begun, strengthened, and sustained. No sin can erase the marks of these sacraments. No matter how far we stray, we cannot change the fact that we belong to Jesus. Given this reality, neither Baptism nor Confirmation can be repeated. The marks they leave on us remain for all eternity.

That being said, mortal sin can stop these marks from having any graced effect in our lives. Mortal sin is deadly sin; it kills the life of God in us. For this reason, sanctifying grace and mortal sin cannot coexist. They are opposites. One is new life and love of God. The other is a turning away from God. Therefore, if or when we commit a mortal sin, the only remedy is repentance in Confession.

The Eucharist

At the Last Supper, Jesus said to his Apostles, "No longer do I call you servants, for the servant does not know what his master is doing; but I have called you friends, for all that I have heard from my Father I have made known to you" (John 15:15). The Sacrament of the Eucharist, which Jesus instituted on the same night he said those words, is the greatest sign of our friendship with God. This is because one of the central truths of friendship is that friends want to be together. We want to talk with them, laugh with them, and simply spend time with them. Friendship with God isn't any different. Jesus couldn't call us to friendship with himself and not make some provision to be with us, his friends (Luke 24:51).

The Eucharist is that provision. It is Jesus Christ, really and substantially present under the guise of bread and wine. In the Eucharist, Jesus abides with us, first on the altar and then in our bodies, just as he promised long ago: "He who eats my flesh and drinks my blood abides in me, and I in him" (John 6:56).

This abiding presence of Jesus was foreshadowed in the Old Covenant by the Passover meal. As their time of captivity in Egypt drew to a close, God commanded the Israelites to eat the Passover, promising that all who partook of it would survive the last and deadliest plague sent upon Egypt. After their liberation, God then commanded the Israelites to celebrate the same Passover meal every year, in memory of how he had liberated them from their captors.

In the New Covenant, the Liturgy of the Eucharist is the new Passover. It is the new event of liberation. It is the new memorial meal (Luke 22:19). It collapses time, re-presenting the events of Calvary to all who participate in the Mass, and allowing us, in a mystical way, to kneel before the Cross of Christ. When we partake of the Eucharistic Jesus, like the ancient Israelites, we are liberated—only our liberation isn't from men, but from the venial sins we have committed. This is one of the reasons why early Christians called the Eucharist the medicine of immortality (John 6:54). All the effects of Jesus' passion and resurrection are communicated to us through the reception of the Eucharist.[1]

The Mass not only makes a past event present, but also reaches forward and touches eternity.[2] In the Mass, we worship Jesus with the entire Church—with all the angels and saints. Mysteriously, the veil between heaven and earth is drawn back, and we enter into the true business of heaven: worship (1 John 3:2).

What we can only sense in part on earth is meant to impel us to seek the full unveiling of the mystery—glory itself. In the Eucharist, the kingdom is here, but not fully. Jesus is here, but not in a manifest way. To see Jesus, one must possess the virtue of faith and accept his words: "this is my body" (Matt 26:26). But as we do so, we hope for the day when we can see him face to face in heaven and realize in full the glory at which the Mass on earth can only hint.

---

[1] Aquinas, ST III, q. 79, a. 1.
[2] Aquinas, ST III, q. 79, a. 2.

For now, in this world, the Eucharist nourishes us spiritually. Just as we need material food to sustain our bodily lives, we need the Eucharist to sustain our spiritual lives—our friendship with Jesus. Everything that material food does for the body the Eucharist does for our souls: it heals us, comforts us, nourishes us, and strengthens us, all the while building us into the ultimate community, the body of Christ, while augmenting and renewing the life of grace given in Baptism.[3]

Ultimately, the Eucharist makes the Church.[4] It is "the source and summit" of its life, uniting people to Jesus and to one another.[5] As St. Paul says:

> The cup of blessing which we bless, is it not a participation in the blood of Christ? The bread which we break, is it not a participation in the body of Christ? Because there is one bread, we who are many are one body, for we all partake of the one bread. (1 Cor 10:16)

This unity is not limited to our time, but extends to all those in purgatory and heaven. This is called the communion of saints. A real unity exists among all the faithful, a unity caused by our gathering around Jesus and our love of God. Because of this unity, all the faithful, living and dead, can truly help one another (CCC p. 249).

The Eucharist not only causes the unity of the Church, but also teaches us what it means to be faithful Catholics and practice the supernatural virtues. The Liturgy of the Word puts us into contact with the model of all virtue, Jesus, as we hear the Word of God. The Liturgy of the Eucharist is God's hospitality and charity poured out for us. It trains us to become more charitable, since in the Eucharist we see Jesus' charity. It also trains us to become more merciful, since in the Eucharist we see Jesus' mercy. This is especially true in our relations to the poor. In the Eucharist, Jesus comes to the spiritually poor—to us— and nourishes us

---

[3] Aquinas, ST III, q. 79, a. 1.

[4] John Paul II, Encyclical Letter on the Eucharist in Its Relationship to the Church *Ecclesia de Eucharistia* (April 17, 2003), §26.

[5] *Lumen Gentium*, §11.

by union with himself. We are called to do the same for all those we meet. In fact, since the Eucharist strengthens our love of Jesus (the virtue of charity), it should fundamentally change the way we view and act in the world. We should see Jesus in all those suffering: the poor, the neglected, the sick, and the outcast (Matt 25:40).

Because the Eucharist is a sign and cause of unity, it is reserved for those who are in full communion with the Church and in good standing—that is, not in a state of serious sin. The Catholic Church considers the lack of unity and the impossibility of intercommunion between Christian denominations a great tragedy, and prays for the day when divisions no longer plague Christians, and all can receive the Eucharist once more.

Just as non-Catholics, who are not united in faith with Catholics, cannot receive the Eucharist, Catholics cannot participate in the communion services of Protestant communities. Those ecclesial communities who find their birth in the Reformation have not preserved the Sacrament of Holy Orders or the fullness of the Eucharistic mystery. The case is different for Orthodox Churches, who have preserved Holy Orders through apostolic succession and therefore celebrate a valid Eucharist.[6] With the proper approvals, Catholics may receive the Eucharist in the Orthodox churches and vice versa. Regardless, in all cases, the Eucharist and the strengthening of the virtue of charity should impel Catholics to pray and work for full unity, just as Jesus prayed that they may all be one (John 17:21).

Penance & Anointing of the Sick

After his resurrection, Jesus entrusted his own power to forgive sins to the Apostles: "If you forgive the sins of any, they are forgiven; if you retain the sins of any, they are retained" (John 20:23). Today, that ministry of forgiveness continues through the Church. The power the Apostles received is the same power their successors—the bishops—and the

---

[6] Second Vatican Council, Decree on Ecumenism *Unitatis Redintegratio* (November 21, 1964), §15.

bishops' helpers—the priests—receive. But the power remains Christ's. Which is why, ultimately, it is Jesus who says to us in the confessional, "your sins are forgiven" (Mark 2:5).

The reality of sin after Baptism is undeniable. Sin damages relationships: our relationships to God, ourselves, reason, and our neighbors. We see this all too often among our families and friends. Sin moves us away from each other. It divides us. When someone lies to us it becomes harder to trust them. When someone betrays us, it is difficult to spend time with them. This also happens, in a sense, in our relationship with Jesus and the Church. Our sins mar our relationship with both. Through our sin, we distance ourselves from them. We pull away from the God who loves us and the Church through which he loves us.

This is especially true with mortal sin. Through mortal sin, we lose God's grace and communion with his Church. Mortal sin is a rejection of both Jesus and the Church. If we continue to reject God until the very end, we suffer eternal punishment: hell. The Sacrament of Reconciliation, however, returns us to the love of God, self, and neighbor. It brings us forgiveness for our sins, heals our relationship with Jesus and the Church, and removes the need for eternal punishment.

What confession does not do, though, is eliminate all the effects of sin on our souls and in the lives of others. If we've told a lie, we have done damage to our soul. We've also done damage to the person or people to whom we lied. Those consequences are real—as real as if we'd taken a knife to our body—and according to justice, the person who sins is still responsible for these consequences (or effects). We must do something or suffer something to make up for what we have done. Just as we might buy flowers for a friend we've hurt—to demonstrate our sorrow, show them we've learned from our mistake, and repair the broken relationship—we also need to make restitution to God for the ways in which we've broken our relationship with him.

This is where temporal punishment comes in. The punishments we are still due for the effects of our sins after confession are called temporal punishment. These punishments aren't inflicted on us by God; they simply follow the very nature of sin.

Traditionally, the Church has identified three ways we can expiate our sins and offer a restitution that satisfies this need for temporal punishment. Prayer is one way. Fasting is another. And almsgiving is a third. Lastly, there is suffering. We can voluntarily endure any evil that befalls us—not complaining needlessly when we are ill or in pain, patiently enduring teasing or insults, and accepting all our crosses with love, then offering them back to God with the same love, joining them, in a sense, to Jesus' suffering on the Cross. This is part of the meaning of redemptive suffering (CCC 1505).

The Sacrament of the Anointing of the Sick is also an important part of overcoming the effects of sin. It not only brings us forgiveness of sins, but also offers spiritual (and sometimes physical healing), plus the grace necessary to suffer well. Anyone who is in danger of death, as well as anyone who is suffering a serious illness, preparing for surgery, or battling a chronic ailment or disability, may (and should) receive this sacrament. Like the Sacrament of Penance and the Eucharist, we can receive it many times throughout the course of our life.

Another way to undo the effects of sin on our souls is to receive an indulgence, which is the partial or total remission of temporal punishment. Just as Jesus could forgive the temporal punishment due to sin, so too can the Church. According to the Catechism:

> An indulgence is obtained through the Church who, by virtue of the power of binding and loosing granted her by Christ Jesus, intervenes in favor of individual Christians and opens for them the treasury of the merits of Christ and the saints to obtain from the Father of mercies the remission of the temporal punishments due for their sins. Thus the Church does not want simply to come to the aid of these Christians, but also to spur them to works of devotion, penance, and charity [Cf. *Indulgentiarum doctrina*, 5]. (CCC 1478)

You can even earn an indulgence for another person, living or deceased.

The moral life is always one lived in community, and this is the primary foundation for the doctrine of indulgences. Nobody lives the moral life alone. The treasury of the Church's graces not only includes the infinite merits of Jesus Christ, but also all those merits Christ has earned through the saints (Col 1:24). These are the merits applied to forgive temporal punishment. This remission, just like every grace, is a gift.

If our temporal punishments are not suffered here or forgiven by an indulgence, then they are suffered in purgatory. Some theologians believe that the fire of purgatory—the fire that purifies all the effects of sin—is the love of Jesus. Pope Benedict XVI explains:

> The encounter with him is the decisive act of judgment. Before his gaze all falsehood melts away. This encounter with him, as it burns us, transforms and frees us, allowing us to become truly ourselves. All that we build during our lives can prove to be mere straw, pure bluster, and it collapses. Yet in the pain of this encounter, when the impurity and sickness of our lives become evident to us, there lies salvation. His gaze, the touch of his heart heals us through an undeniably painful transformation "as through fire." But it is a blessed pain, in which the holy power of his love sears through us like a flame, enabling us to become totally ourselves and thus totally of God.[7]

Marriage and Holy Orders

The sacraments of initiation and penance allow us to begin living lives of grace and help us to grow in Christian maturity. God has given them to us to sustain and restore our earthly happiness and give us a foretaste of eternal happiness. There also are sacraments for specific vocations: namely, marriage and Holy Orders. These exist not for the holiness of those receiving them (although that can happen too), but rather for the mission of the Church and the holiness and supernatural happiness of others. Often called "sacraments at the service of the communion," these sacraments offer the

---

[7] Benedict XVI, Encyclical Letter on Christian Hope *Spe Salvi* (November 30, 2007), §47.

grace necessary to serve others and build up the Church.

Holy Orders is the vital link between the grace of Christ and our moral lives (CCC 1536). The sacraments, remember, are the means through which God communicates his forgiving and sustaining grace to us. But without Holy Orders, there would be no sacraments. There would be no concrete, visible, tangible, and historical link to Jesus himself.

Humans are communal, material, and historical beings. Thus, it makes perfect sense that Jesus would choose bishops (and priests to aid them) to continue his mission and communicate his life. It also makes perfect sense that Jesus would choose to communicate that life through the sacraments, which are visible, historical, concrete, and tangible effective signs of his grace. Humans are not disembodied spirits trapped in a body; we are a union of body and soul. Likewise, humans are not isolated individuals; we are communal creatures, made to live in society. Thus, our supernatural salvation comes in a historical way, through historical individuals, and communal liturgical events.

Furthermore, inasmuch as the life of supernatural virtue centers on Jesus, it centers on the Eucharist. The moral life is born of the Eucharistic sacrifice and returns through it to praise God. The Eucharist requires a priesthood. It is a sacrifice, and only priests can offer sacrifice. This does not mean that the numerically singular sacrifice of Jesus is added to by the sacrifice of the Mass. Rather, it means that the one sacrifice of Jesus is continually offered in and through the Mass (CCC 1545). Of this sacrifice, the life of supernatural virtue is born.

Marriage is also essential to the Church. The Sacrament of Marriage is Jesus forming a small cell of his Church—we call this cell the "domestic church"—so that the spouses can grow strong, serve others, and in turn strengthen the whole Church. Through the sacrament, couples receive the grace they need to love one another, form their children, and serve the wider community. By grace, marriage is the first school of virtue and catechesis for all Christians. Living in the community of our family, we learn how to love, pray, forgive, and serve others. We also learn about the love Jesus has for his Church, seeing in the enduring, fruitful, faithful love of husband and wife an image of Jesus and his Bride.

Husbands, love your wives, as Christ loved the Church and gave himself up for her, that he might sanctify her, having cleansed her by the washing of water with the word, that he might present the church to himself in splendor, without spot or wrinkle or any such thing, that she might be holy and without blemish. Even so husbands should love their wives as their own bodies. He who loves his wife loves himself. For no man ever hates his own flesh, but nourishes and cherishes it, as Christ does the Church, because we are members of his body. "For this reason a man shall leave his father and mother and be joined to his wife, and the two shall become one flesh." This is a great mystery, and I mean in reference to Christ and the Church; however, let each one of you love his wife as himself, and let the wife see that she respects her husband. (Eph 5:25–31)

SELECTED READING
Second Vatican Council, Constitution on the Sacred Liturgy
Sacrosanctum Concilium (December 4, 1963), nos. 5–7

God who "wills that all men be saved and come to the knowledge of the truth" (1 Tim. 2:4), "who in many and various ways spoke in times past to the fathers by the prophets" (Heb. 1:1), when the fullness of time had come sent His Son, the Word made flesh, anointed by the Holy Spirit, to preach the gospel to the poor, to heal the contrite of heart, to be a "bodily and spiritual medicine," the Mediator between God and man. For His humanity, united with the person of the Word, was the instrument of our salvation. Therefore in Christ "the perfect achievement of our reconciliation came forth, and the fullness of divine worship was given to us."

The wonderful works of God among the people of the Old Testament were but a prelude to the work of Christ the Lord in redeeming mankind and giving perfect glory to God. He achieved His task principally by the paschal mystery of His blessed passion, resurrection from the dead, and the glorious ascension, whereby "dying, he destroyed our death and, rising, he restored our life." For it was from the side of Christ as He slept the sleep of death upon the cross that there came forth "the wondrous sacrament of the whole Church."

Just as Christ was sent by the Father, so also He sent the apostles, filled with the Holy Spirit. This He did that, by preaching the gospel to every creature, they might proclaim that the Son of God, by His death and resurrection, had freed us from the power of Satan and from death, and brought us into the kingdom of His Father. His purpose also was that they might accomplish the work of salvation which they had proclaimed, by means of sacrifice and sacraments, around which the entire liturgical life revolves. Thus by baptism men are plunged into the paschal mystery of Christ: they die with Him, are buried with Him, and rise with Him; they receive the spirit of adoption as sons "in which we cry: Abba, Father" (Rom. 8:15), and thus become true adorers whom the Father seeks. In like manner, as often as they eat the supper of the Lord they proclaim the death of the Lord until He comes. For that reason, on the very day of Pentecost, when the Church appeared before the world, "those who received the word" of Peter "were baptized." And "they continued steadfastly in the teaching of the apostles and in the communion of the breaking of bread and in prayers . . . praising God and being in favor with all the people" (Acts 2:41–47). From that time onwards the Church has never failed to come together to celebrate the paschal mystery: reading those things "which were in all the scriptures concerning him" (Luke 24:27), celebrating the Eucharist in which "the victory and triumph of his death are again made present," and at the same time giving thanks "to God for his unspeakable gift" (2 Cor. 9:15) in Christ Jesus, "in praise of his glory" (Eph. 1:12), through the power of the Holy Spirit.

To accomplish so great a work, Christ is always present in His Church, especially in her liturgical celebrations. He is present in the sacrifice of the Mass, not only in the person of His minister, "the same now offering, through the ministry of priests, who formerly offered himself on the cross," but especially under the Eucharistic species. By His power He is present in the sacraments, so that when a man baptizes it is really Christ Himself who baptizes. He is present in His word, since it is He Himself who speaks when the holy scriptures are read in the Church. He is present, lastly, when the Church prays and sings, for He promised: "Where two or three are gathered together in my name, there am I in the midst of them" (Matt. 18:20).

Christ indeed always associates the Church with Himself in this great work wherein God is perfectly glorified and men are sanctified. The Church is His beloved Bride who calls to her Lord, and through Him offers worship to the Eternal Father.

Rightly, then, the liturgy is considered as an exercise of the priestly office of Jesus Christ. In the liturgy the sanctification of the man is signified by signs perceptible to the senses, and is effected in a way which corresponds with each of these signs; in the liturgy the whole public worship is performed by the Mystical Body of Jesus Christ, that is, by the Head and His members.

From this it follows that every liturgical celebration, because it is an action of Christ the priest and of His Body which is the Church, is a sacred action surpassing all others; no other action of the Church can equal its efficacy by the same title and to the same degree.

QUESTIONS FOR REVIEW

1. What are the sacraments of initiation?
2. How does the Sacrament of Confirmation aid us in answering God's call to holiness?
3. Which sacrament nourishes our souls with sanctifying grace?
4. Which sacraments help us overcome the effects of sin in our lives?
5. What are the sacraments at the service of communion? How do they help the Body of Christ?

QUESTIONS FOR DISCUSSION

1. Which sacraments have you received? How many of these do you remember receiving? Which sacrament stands out as being particularly memorable or important when you received it? Why?

2. How often do you receive the Eucharist or spend time with Jesus in Eucharistic adoration? How might making a special effort to receive the Eucharist more or pray more frequently in front of the Blessed Sacrament help you?

3. Do you struggle with going to Confession, are you grateful for it, or a little bit of both? How do you feel before going to Confession? How do you feel afterward?

Chapter 4

OTHER HELPS

Our Vocation

As we discussed in Part I, each of us has a vocation—or "calling"—to holiness. Ultimately, God made each of us for the same purpose: sainthood. He created us for an eternally joyful relationship with him. This call to holiness is often described as our universal vocation. No matter who we are, where we come from, or what we've done, we have this calling.

Likewise, for each of us answering this call requires participating in Jesus Christ's priestly, prophetic, and kingly mission. As the Catechism explains:

> Jesus Christ is the one whom the Father anointed with the Holy Spirit and established as priest, prophet, and king. The whole People of God participates in these three offices of Christ and bears the responsibilities for mission and service that flow from them [Cf. John Paul II, *RH* 21–18]. (CCC 783)

Because Jesus came to offer himself as an atoning sacrifice for our sins (an offering that he continues to make eternally in heaven), Jesus has a priestly mission. He is, in fact, our "great high priest" (Heb 4:14). Likewise, because he came to announce the kingdom of God, he has a prophetic mission. And, because he rules over that kingdom, he has a kingly mission; he is the "King of kings and Lord of lords" (Rev 19:16).

Because we have been joined to Jesus Christ in Baptism, each of us shares in this three-fold ministry of his. Each of us is called to exercise a form of baptismal priesthood—offering ourselves and our world to the Lord. We are, in effect, consecrated to God's service; and when we strive to make everything we do an offering for him—our work, our play, our relationships, and our suffering—and seek to glorify him in all things, we participate in his priestly ministry (CCC 1546).

So too, we all are called to participate in his prophetic ministry by preaching the Gospel and calling others to repentance. When we proclaim the truth in word and deed—standing up for what's right and showing others how to live by our example—we serve God as prophets in our schools, homes, workplaces, and community.

Finally, all of us participate in Christ's kingly office. Each of us has been entrusted with the task of ruling over ourselves—exercising the virtues so that we can live fruitful, joyful, well-ordered lives. We also continue to exercise stewardship over creation. By justly, prudently, and charitably carrying out our responsibilities over ourselves, over others (when we are in positions of authority), and over all the things God has entrusted to us—our homes, rooms, possessions, etc.—we share in Christ's kingly ministry.

For the laity especially, it remains our sacred task to carry out these functions in the world. Our special sphere of responsibility is all that lies outside of the Church's doors—from classrooms to playing fields. The Catechism notes that Vatican II teaches:

> "By reason of their special vocation it belongs to the laity to seek the kingdom of God by engaging in temporal affairs and directing them according to God's will. . . . It pertains to them in a special way so as to illuminate and order all temporal things with which they are closely associated that these may always be effected and grow according to Christ and may be to the glory of the Creator and Redeemer" [LG 31 § 2]. (CCC 898)

The Primary Vocation

Although all Christians share in these tasks by virtue of our universal vocation to holiness, we share in them in different ways depending upon our state in life, three of which are often called the primary or spousal vocations.

Our primary vocation is really about the relationship through which each of us pursues our universal vocation to holiness. Traditionally, the Church holds up three different primary vocations: marriage, priesthood, and consecrated life.

Those who are called to marriage journey to holiness through the trials and tribulations of marriage and family life. Husbands and wives vow themselves "until death do us part" to each other and lay down their lives for one another, helping each other answer God's call to holiness (CCC 1603).

Those who are called to the priesthood also make a solemn vow; they pledge themselves to serve the Bride of Christ, the Church. In effect, they take Christ's Bride as their own. It is for Christ's Bride that priests lay down their lives, and through that relationship—through service to the Church—the priest grows closer to God and answers his call to holiness (CCC 1555).

Finally, those who are called to the consecrated vocation—whether as religious brothers and sisters, hermits, or consecrated virgins—solemnly vow to take Christ as their spouse now. The whole of their life—body and soul—is consecrated to his service. Through that total gift of self to Jesus in this life, they too walk the long road to heaven and answer the universal call to holiness (CCC 914).

Oftentimes, lay people live their universal vocations with the help of an organized community or movement. For example, an Italian priest named Luigi Guisanni founded Communion and Liberation. Communion and Liberation involves people in all states of life forming communities in order to advance in holiness and promote the mission of the Church. Other laity choose to associate themselves with those living the consecrated vocation, both to imitate their charism and seek holiness with them. These are called the third orders, in the case of the Dominicans, Franciscans, or Carmelites, and oblates in the case of the Benedictines.

Particular Vocations

If our universal vocation is our ultimate destiny—where we are going—and our primary vocation is a relationship that helps us attain that destiny, our particular vocation to service is what we do as we journey to holiness. It's what God calls each of us as individuals to do in order to exercise our priestly, prophetic, and kingly ministry. It represents how we serve him and others in this world.

Many of us offer this service this through our work. God calls some people to make the Kingdom of God manifest in the world through their service as doctors or nurses, teachers or lawyers, politicians or artists. Through the natural gifts he gives us and the opportunities he provides, he truly calls us to serve him and others through our work. The Fathers of the Second Vatican Council address the value of work to the pursuit of holiness in *Gaudium et Spes*, writing:

> Just as [human activity] proceeds from man, so it is ordered towards man. For when a man works he not only alters things and society, he develops himself as well. He learns much, he cultivates his resources, he goes outside of himself and beyond himself. Rightly understood, this kind of growth is of greater value than any external riches which can be garnered. . . . Hence, the norm of human activity is this: that in accord with the divine plan and will, it should harmonize with the genuine good of the human race, and that it allow people as individuals and as members of society to pursue their total vocation and fulfill it.[1]

God can also call us to serve him in countless other ways, including through our suffering—allowing us to join our sufferings to his and helping "complete" his work of redemption.[2] Others he may call to serve him through missionary work—preaching the Gospel through words

---

[1] *Lumen Gentium*, §35.
[2] John Paul II, Encyclical Letter on the Christian Meaning of Human Suffering *Salvifici Doloris*, §23.

and actions around the world—or through apostolates of service—working with the materially or spiritually poor, helping to end abortion, or defending the truth about marriage (CCC 863). All of us are called to serve him as men and women, living out the masculine and feminine vocation, with love (CCC 2392).

Right now, you, too, have a particular vocation. God is calling you to serve him through your vocation as a student and a single person. When you commit yourself to your studies, doing your best to take advantage of the educational opportunities you have and learning all you can so that you can someday serve God in another way, you are giving him glory and answering his call. Likewise, when you embrace your current unmarried state, using this time to develop strong, chaste friendships and grow in faith, you're also glorifying God and answering his call to you in this moment of your life. Like with all the particular vocations, God gives you actual graces to carry out the duties of your present state and cope with the struggles of the present moment. When you receive those graces and seek to answer this call, your service to him helps you grow in holiness. It helps you live the good life.

Each of the vocations discussed above matters. Each is important. None is dispensable. As St. Paul says:

> For just as the body is one and has many members, and all the members of the body though many, are one body, so it is with Christ. For by one Spirit we were all baptized into one body—Jews or Greeks, slaves or free—and all were made to drink of one Spirit. For the body does not consist of one member but of many. . . . But as it is, God arranged the organs in the body, each one of them, as he chose. (1 Cor 12:12–13, 18)

The Help of the Holy Spirit

When it comes to growing in love and virtue and answering God's call to holiness, none of us do it on our own. It is not primarily about us buckling down and just working harder at "being good." Discipline and effort, of course, are necessary. Thinking through questions of right and wrong with the help of our reason is a must. Nevertheless, when it comes to becoming the men and women God made us to be, the bulk of the work is done by the Holy Spirit.

It is the Holy Spirit who conforms us to the Son. It is the Holy Spirit who dwells in us through the virtue of charity. And it is the Holy Spirit who provides us with the gifts that help us to receive and carry out his guidance in the supernatural life, so that we can abide in supernatural happiness.

The gifts of the Holy Spirit are habits that make us docile to God's guidance in our life (CCC 1830–1831). With these gifts, God's guidance is not violent or imposed from the outside. Rather, the gifts of the Holy Spirit help us to long for God's guidance so that we both welcome it and promptly follow it.

In total, there are seven gifts of the Holy Spirit: wisdom, understanding, counsel, fortitude, knowledge, piety, and fear of the Lord. Each of these prepare our minds, hearts, and emotions to be moved by God. Through the gifts of wisdom, understanding, and knowledge, our fundamental vision of the world and God is changed. We learn to see the world more as it really is. God's wisdom and knowledge informs and shapes our own. The gifts of wisdom, understanding, and knowledge are thus the very roots of theology, which move us to judge all in light of God (wisdom), understand the articles of the creed (understanding), and reason about action and the world based on that understanding and wisdom (knowledge). In turn, counsel (the ability to see the best way to follow God's plan), piety (true devotion), fear of the Lord (awe and amazement at God's perfections), and fortitude (the ability to do what's right even when it's difficult), help us to live what we see. They enable us to do the good we know we ought to do.

When we are moved by God according to the gifts of the Holy Spirit and act out of our supernatural virtues, we see signs of this in our lives. These are called the fruits of the Spirit. The fruits of the Spirit are charity, joy, peace, patience, kindness, goodness, generosity, gentleness, faithfulness, modesty, self-control, and chastity (CCC 1832).

These fruits are the consequences of loving God, receiving his grace, and cooperating with his guidance as we make choices, both big and small. How we treat our parents, our siblings, and the weakest among us; how we behave at school and on the playing field; how we behave and think about the poor and our enemies; how we act around those who aren't popular or who are cruel to us; even how we behave behind the wheel of a car are all occasions for cooperating with God's guidance. The more we cooperate, the more it shows in both our hearts and actions.

Conscience

When making moral decisions, one of the most important helps we can have at our disposal is a well-formed conscience. What does this mean, though?

The Nature of Conscience

Conscience is a word that gets tossed around frequently in modern Western society. Even atheists speak of following their conscience. But few people actually know what the word means. We simply adopt the typical usage from our culture (which itself adopted it from Christianity). The problem is that our culture didn't just adopt the word conscience from Christianity; it also transformed the meaning of the word. Hence, before we can understand why the Church teaches that we should form our consciences in light of her teachings, we first need to understand what a conscience is.

Essentially, conscience is a judgment of reason about the moral quality of a concrete action. It's not feeling. It's a decision guided by prudence. Even in a fallen world, most of us still know that some things are good and some things are evil. The natural law, which is ordered to our nature, helps us see this. Our conscience, in turn, helps us apply that knowledge of right and wrong to particular decisions. For this reason, conscience is often called the voice of God. God speaks through our natures and through the primary principles of natural law. Without God, our consciences would have no authority. Hence, John Henry Cardinal

Newman says that:

> Conscience is a law of the mind; yet [Christians] would not
> grant that it is nothing more; I mean that it was not a dictate, nor
> conveyed the notion of responsibility, of duty, of a threat and
> a promise. . . . [Conscience] is a messenger of him, who, both
> in nature and in grace, speaks to us behind a veil, and teaches
> and rules us by his representatives. Conscience is the aboriginal
> Vicar of Christ.[3]

The Formation of Conscience

However, none of this means that our conscience is always and automatically right. It's not. Our consciences can lead us astray. In order to prevent that, we have to form it, just like we form our bodies to perform certain tasks. Think, for example, of baseball players, who have to practice long and hard before they can hit fast balls or catch line drives consistently and easily. Eventually, their bodies can perform those tasks without much thought. That's because of the training they put themselves through.

In a similar way, we have to "train" our consciences so that they can consistently and easily direct us to a good end. A well-formed conscience can choose the good with the same ease that Babe Ruth hit home runs; it becomes, eventually, almost an automatic response.

Why do we need to form our consciences at all, though? First, because it is an act of our minds concerning the truth. None of us are omniscient or infallible. Our minds have been darkened by sin. Concupiscence makes it difficult for us to always perceive what's best. This means our conscience can be wrong. In order to be right, it has to be in conformity with reality, in conformity with the truth of the human person, and in conformity with the good. In order to learn these things, we must allow others to teach us. This is what it means to form our con-

---

[3] John Henry Cardinal Newman, "Letter to the Duke of Norfolk," V, in *Certain Difficulties felt by Anglicans in Catholic Teaching* II (London: Longmans Green, 1885), 248. Quoted in CCC 1778.

science. It means that we let someone else shape our decision-making capabilities, our very judgments about what is good and bad.

But who? To whom do we look for guidance about right and wrong? That's the real question. All of us, whether we realize it or not, form our conscience in accord with someone else's direction. For a lot of people, that someone else is the culture. We take in what the people on television or in the magazines say about right and wrong. Then, we act in accord with what we see, hear, and read. The problem with this is that the culture is often wrong about the most important questions. Like us, the people shaping our culture struggle with concupiscence and all its negative effects. The same holds true for our friends. Our friends may be great, but they're not God. They're not going to see everything as they should, and listening to them might get us in as much trouble as listening to the advice of our favorite pop singer.

This is why we need the Church. As the Body of Christ, the Church claims the primary place in forming our consciences. She is the one entrusted by God with the tasks of preserving, guarding, and interpreting divine Revelation. She is the one with the charism of infallibility, which ensures that she never teaches error in her dogmas. While individual members of the Church may struggle, the magisterium provides us with a sure and steady guide. When we study the Church's teachings about the moral life, when we read Sacred Scripture, the writings of the saints, and books by wise teachers, we form our consciences in accord with the truth. We are, in effect, training our consciences to give us good guidance that we can trust.

Following Our Conscience

It is within this vision of conscience that we have to situate the Church's teaching that we should always follow our consciences (CCC 1782). The Church recognizes conscience as the ultimate arbiter for each of us about what course of action we should take. Our popular culture has kept this teaching, but substituted a different view of conscience, one in which conscience is simply an inner voice, a feeling, or a way of being "true" to one's self.

This is not what the Church means when she tells us to follow our conscience. If your friends are all getting drunk on Saturday night, your feelings may incline you to join them. You want to be a part of what they're doing. If, however, you've formed your conscience in accord with truth, you know that despite those feelings, getting drunk is wrong. The more alcohol you consume, the more it diminishes your capacity to make reasonable decisions. This knowledge, not your feelings, is what needs to guide your actions.

Conscience is the ultimate guide for each of us. We must always do what our conscience says we must do. If you think something is wrong and do it anyway, you condemn yourself with your own actions. If you think something is right and fail to do it, you do the same.

Again, though, this doesn't mean your conscience is never wrong. When we judge sincerely but incorrectly, this is called an erroneous conscience. Depending on why we've judged incorrectly, we may not be at fault for making a wrong decision. Our ignorance of the truth could be involuntary. This is called invincible ignorance. If you are invincibly ignorant it means you are not at fault for your ignorance, so you also are not guilty of the bad actions that follow from your ignorance.

For example, if someone has been raised in a home and community that is so hostile to or ignorant of Christianity that they've never been exposed to Jesus and his teachings, that person wouldn't be guilty of making bad decisions based on an improperly formed conscience. But if a person has freely chosen not to learn about Jesus or what the Church teaches, they have what the Church calls vincible ignorance. This means they are at fault for their ignorance and, consequently, for their erroneous conscience.

It's also possible that someone could be so emmeshed in their sins or so entrapped by certain vices that even though they've been exposed to the truth, their sins and vices lead them astray, confounding their judgement and making them think that evil is good and good is evil. This is why it's so important that we work hard to cultivate the human virtues and stay close to the sacraments, which nurture the supernatural virtues within us. The more we grow in grace and virtue, the less susceptible we are to bad judgments rooted in our own sin.

While an erroneous conscience is a hindrance to living a joyful, well-ordered life now and attaining eternal happiness with God in heaven, a well-formed conscience is a tremendous help. It guides us in decisions both big and small, helping us to live according to God's loving law and to love others as he made us to do. A well-formed conscience always speaks to us—sometimes quietly, sometimes loudly—urging us to do the right thing, calling us away from the wrong thing, and keeping us on the path that leads to life.

Regular Habits of Prayer

Everything we've talked about in Part IV so far is essential to living good and joyful lives. Without the virtues, grace, the sacraments, the Holy Spirit, and a well-formed conscience, we can't become the men and women God made us to be. We can't live the lives he made us to live or love the people he made us to love. One thread binds together all these different types of "helps": a regular habit of prayer, both on our own and in the community of the faithful—that is, in the Mass.

As a commentary on the Rule of St. Benedict says, "Just as breathing is always necessary for the continuation of life in the body, so is prayer absolutely essential for spiritual health . . . I would more easily believe that a man has no soul than that he could become perfect without prayer."[4] This is why 1 Thessalonians 5:17 urges us to "pray constantly." The importance of prayer for the virtuous life is hard to overrate. What, however, is prayer?

The Nature of Prayer

One of the most basic definitions of prayer comes to us from the great Doctor of the Church St. John Damascene, who defines prayer as "the

---

[4] Quoted in Dominic Prummer, O.P., *Handbook of Moral Theology,* trans. Gerald Shelton (Cork: The Mercier Press, 1956), 169.

raising of the mind to God."⁵ We can do this "raising" by talking to God, listening to God, singing to God, thinking of God, or carrying out an action to honor God. When we talk to God, we can use our own words or the words of a more formal prayer, like the Our Father or the Hail Mary. We can have long conversations or short conversations with him. We can pray in bed, in the car, on a walk, or in Church. Basically, we can talk to God anywhere, about anything, in any way that helps us share our heart with him.

From this basic approach to prayer, the Church breaks it down a bit more, identifying four general types of prayer: adoration, petition, intercession, and thanksgiving. When we raise our minds to God in adoration, we acknowledge that he is infinite goodness and worthy of all our love. Petition is when we raise our minds to God and ask for something from him, the giver of all good gifts; this could include forgiveness, assistance in making a decision, help finding a spouse, strength for carrying out his will, or a material need like food, a job, or physical healing. Intercession is when we raise our minds to God and ask for the needs of others; we ask God to heal someone else, guide someone else, help someone else. Finally, thanksgiving is when we raise our minds to God and offer him thanks. This can be a long prayer of thanks or it can be a quick thought of gratitude as we see a beautiful sunset or eat a delicious ice cream sundae.

In addition to these four types of prayers, the Church gives us many different ways we can offer these prayers to God. One way is meditation (CCC 2708). Christian meditation is not sitting on the floor with our legs crossed and chanting "ohm." It's using our minds to think about the truths of the faith. We can begin our meditation by studying the Scriptures, reading the writings of the saints or other teachers of the faith, contemplating creation, praying the Rosary, or looking at a religious image. We then think deeply about the words we've read, the words we've said, or what we see in front of us. This mental engagement with truth is prayer, for it raises our minds to God and allows him to show us things

---

⁵ St. John Damascene, "Prayer is the raising of one's mind and heart to God or the requesting of good things from God," *Defide orth.* 3, 24: PG 94, 1089C; quoted in CCC 2559.

we might not have seen on our own.

Likewise, prayer can be vocal or mental. We can pray aloud or silently. We can form words in our head, or simply allow ourselves to feel the presence of God. Both are fitting in different circumstances. Both reflect the truth of the human person, who is a union of spirit and flesh, and who therefore prays in the spirit and the flesh. Expressions of the body also denote a type of prayer and intention to pray. Kneeling, for example, is a way of showing God we recognize our dependence on him and feel awe in his presence. Likewise, standing denotes the joy of the resurrection, of standing in the risen Christ, which is one of the reasons we stand when the Gospel is read in Mass.[6]

Contemplative prayer is in some sense the purest form of prayer and should permeate the above styles and types of prayer. St. Teresa of Ávila defines contemplative prayer as "nothing else than a close sharing between friends; it means taking time frequently to be alone with him who we know loves us."[7] Contemplative prayer recollects us and dedicates all of us—the entirety of our being—to loving contemplation of God and his activity. It is prayer in silence, a prayer beyond words. It is union with the prayer of Christ, being taken up into Christ's perfect prayer. From this core, this silence of love, the person then draws the strength and grace to live the virtuous life (CCC 2709–2719).

For all the different forms prayer can take, at its most basic, prayer is a communion, a uniting with God in love. Hence, it is possible to "pray constantly." As the virtue of charity grows to perfection in us, our very being becomes a prayer. For the saint, everything they say and do is a prayer. Their hearts glorify God in every activity.

The Purpose of Prayer

So, that's what prayer is and can be. But what does prayer do? After all, doesn't Jesus say, "your Father knows what you need before you ask him"

---

[6] Benedict XVI, *Spirit of the Liturgy* (San Francisco: Ignatius Press, 2014), 194.

[7] Teresa of Jesus, *The Book of Her Life*, 8.5, in *The Collected Works of St. Teresa of Avila*, trans. Kieran Kavanaugh, OCD, and Otilio Rodriguez, OCD (Washington DC: Institute of Carmelite Studies, 1976), 1:67. Quoted in CCC 2709.

(Matt 6:8)? Why should we bother praying if Jesus already knows what we need and what we feel?

First, we should remember this objection only applies to prayers of petition and intercession, forgetting that adoration and thanksgiving are also essential forms of prayer. Second, we need to remember that Jesus himself commanded us to petition God, asking him for our "daily bread" (Matt 6:11). We ask God for help, for grace, and to meet our needs because Jesus said we should. God wants us to come to him. God wants us to recognize our dependence on him. God wants us to trust him with our hearts and our lives, and one of the ways we give him that trust is by asking him for what our hearts desire.

Regular prayer, whether of intercession, adoration, petition, or thanksgiving, puts us in close, intimate contact with Jesus. It draws us closer to him, helping us to know him better as we freely share more of ourselves with him. Like any relationship, our relationship with God depends on contact. We can't grow closer to him if we don't spend time with him, talk to him, acknowledge his gifts, and praise him for his goodness. Simply put, spending time in prayer with the one who made us changes us into the person we were made to be.

Prayer doesn't just change us; as St. Thomas Aquinas said, prayer also changes things.[8] It is not that prayer changes God; God can't change. He's God. But, God, who rules all things, does bring about effects (sometimes miraculous effects) through our prayers. He both causes us to pray through his grace and brings about an effect that is beyond our power. Basically, he makes our prayers powerful. By his grace, we get to participate in his providence.

This is true for us, who still live on earth, and it's even more true of the saints, who live forever with God in heaven. This is one of the reasons why we, as Catholics, call upon the intercession of the saints. When we pray "to" the saints, what we're really asking them to do is pray for us. We do this because we know that the saints have a greater friendship with God. Their intercession, because of that friendship and merit, is more efficacious.

This is preeminently true of the Blessed Virgin Mary (John 2:3–5).

---

[8] Aquinas, ST II-II, q. 83, a. 2.

Mary is the mother of Jesus, but she also is the mother of all believers. Jesus established this relationship while he hung upon the Cross, telling the beloved disciple (who represents the whole Christian community), "Behold, your mother!" (John 19:25–27). Far from simply making sure Mary has a place to stay, Jesus' words put the whole Christian community in a filial relationship to Mary. Jesus is the son of Mary. The Christian community is sent to continue his mission and stands in his place. Moreover, through Baptism, we are configured to Christ. We become part of his body. Thus, the Christian community is also a child of Mary. Mary is both part of the Church and mother of the Church. These two roles cannot be separated.

Since prayer is always expressed through the Church, prayer in and through Mary, who is mother and image of the Church, is powerful and transformative. Mary, on account of her special graces and special place in the economy of salvation, teaches us to perfectly abandon ourselves to God by placing our lives in her hands. In a very real sense praying with and through Mary puts us in touch with the very heart of the Church's prayer.[9]

Remember, though: prayer is only in and through the Church because it is in and through Christ. The mediation of Christ includes and utilizes the mediation of the Church and the saints. Christ's sacrifice is inclusive and enabling of others; it does not exclude other sacrifices or render them without value. In fact, it is through Christ's sacrifice and mediation that other sacrifices and mediations take on value. The sacrifices and prayers of the saints "complete what is lacking in Christ's afflictions for the sake of his body, that is, the Church" (Col 1:24) because "it is no longer I who live but Christ who lives in me" (Gal 2:20). This is the great truth of the Christian life, a truth lived most fully by Mary but also lived by all of us who seek to conform our life to Christ's. In his mercy, he invites all into his perfect prayer, and he makes our works and prayers meritorious and effective by his power.

---

[9] John Paul II, Post-Synodal Apostolic Exhortation on the Encounter with the Living Jesus Christ: The Way to Conversion, Communion and Solidarity in America *Ecclesia in America* (January 22, 1999), §10.

This happens preeminently in the Mass, the place where we enter most perfectly into the prayer and meditation of Christ.

The Mass is the perfect form and model of prayer. It is the whole Church gathered in and through Christ's grace to join him in eternally praising the Father. Likewise, in the Mass, Jesus makes himself truly present to us in the Eucharist. Jesus is not just with us in spirit in the Mass; he is with us in the flesh. He then gives himself to us, Body to body. This act of communion anticipates the ultimate act of communion, the ultimate prayer, to which God calls us in heaven.

In all these ways, the Mass communicates essential graces for the good life. Accordingly, to miss Mass voluntarily, for less than the most serious of reasons, is a mortal sin. When we don't participate in the Mass regularly and reverently, we miss the chance to pray with the Body of Christ, and we miss the chance to receive the Body of Christ. We turn our back on the most powerful of prayers and the greatest of gifts. In effect, we reject the love and grace offered to us, the love and grace necessary for spiritual growth and maturity. And that is a tragic loss.

Holding Fast

On the long road to sainthood, the surest help and guide we have is Jesus Christ. On the one hand, the adage, "What would Jesus do?" is rarely applicable to the rest of us; Jesus is God—all knowing, all loving, without sin—so he can know more and do more than any of the rest of us. He is inimitable. Nevertheless, it's still vital that we constantly meditate upon Jesus' teachings and life. In his earthly life and his activity through the saints, he demonstrates what it means to have the supernatural virtues. He shows us what they look like in action. As such, we must constantly return to his life, search his teachings, and appropriate his example.

We also must ask him for the gift of perseverance (CCC 2849). Just as human friendships can fail, so too can our friendship with God. We can sin. We can turn our back on God.

There's an old saying that reminds us that "sin makes you stupid." That is, sin can harden our hearts and darken our vision. The deeper we journey into a life of sin, the harder it becomes to see the truth, let alone live in truth. We can't see truth because we live in darkness, and we don't want to see it because that would mean changing our lives. Every step toward sin puts our souls in mortal danger—not because God won't forgive us . . . but because eventually, we may not want that forgiveness. Instead of wanting the things that will bring us life, love, and happiness, we will want only what will bring us death, sorrow, and eternal loneliness.

Following the way of Christ is the road to true freedom. It's also the road to becoming who God made us to be—absolutely unique, unrepeatable, one of a kind images of God. Sinners think they're unique, but sin really robs us of our personality. It makes us less "us" and more like our sin. Sanctity restores the uniqueness of our personality. It draws out all of our gifts and helps us use them for the greater glory of God. We see this most clearly in the rich variety of saints.

The fiery St. Jerome, the brilliant St. Thomas, the brave St. Joan, the passionate St. Catherine, the humble St. Francis and the tireless St. Teresa all glorify God. All are examples of what it means to possess the supernatural virtues in Christ. All took advantage of all the helps God offers. They grew in virtue, opened themselves up to grace, stayed close to God in the sacraments, listened to the Holy Spirit, formed their conscience in accord with the Church's teaching, and prayed constantly. Their reward was that they got to be really and truly themselves, really and truly free, forever enjoying God's friendship in heaven.

If we follow their example, our reward will be the same.

SELECTED READING
Second Vatican Council, Dogmatic Constitution on the Church *Lumen Gentium* (November 21, 1964), nos. 31–33

The term laity is here understood to mean all the faithful except those in holy orders and those in the state of religious life specially approved by the Church. These faithful are by baptism made one body with Christ and are constituted among the People of God; they are in their own way made sharers in the priestly, prophetical, and kingly functions of Christ; and they carry out for their own part the mission of the whole Christian people in the Church and in the world.

What specifically characterizes the laity is their secular nature. It is true that those in holy orders can at times be engaged in secular activities, and even have a secular profession. But they are by reason of their particular vocation especially and professedly ordained to the sacred ministry. Similarly, by their state in life, religious give splendid and striking testimony that the world cannot be transformed and offered to God without the spirit of the beatitudes. But the laity, by their very vocation, seek the kingdom of God by engaging in temporal affairs and by ordering them according to the plan of God. They live in the world, that is, in each and in all of the secular professions and occupations. They live in the ordinary circumstances of family and social life, from which the very web of their existence is woven. They are called there by God that by exercising their proper function and led by the spirit of the Gospel they may work for the sanctification of the world from within as a leaven. In this way they may make Christ known to others, especially by the testimony of a life resplendent in faith, hope and charity. Therefore, since they are tightly bound up in all types of temporal affairs it is their special task to order and to throw light upon these affairs in such a way that they may come into being and then continually increase according to Christ to the praise of the Creator and the Redeemer.

By divine institution Holy Church is ordered and governed with a wonderful diversity. "For just as in one body we have many members, yet all the members have not the same function, so we, the many, are one body in Christ, but severally members one of another." Therefore, the chosen People of God is one: "one Lord, one faith, one baptism"; sharing a common dignity as members from their regeneration in Christ, having the same filial grace and the same vocation to perfection; possessing in common one salvation, one hope and one undivided charity. There is, therefore, in Christ and in the Church no inequality on the basis of race or nationality, social condition or sex, because "there is neither Jew nor Greek: there is neither bond nor free: there is neither male nor female. For you are all 'one' in Christ Jesus."

If therefore in the Church everyone does not proceed by the same path, nevertheless all are called to sanctity and have received an equal privilege of faith through the justice of God. And if by the will of Christ some are made teachers, pastors and dispensers of mysteries on behalf of others, yet all share a true equality with regard to the dignity and to the activity common to all the faithful for the building up of the Body of Christ. For the distinction which the Lord made between sacred ministers and the rest of the People of God bears within it a certain union, since pastors and the other faithful are bound to each other by a mutual need. Pastors of the Church, following the example of the Lord, should minister to one another and to the other faithful. These in their turn should enthusiastically lend their joint assistance to their pastors and teachers. Thus in their diversity all bear witness to the wonderful unity in the Body of Christ. This very diversity of graces, ministries and works gathers the children of God into one, because "all these things are the work of one and the same Spirit."

Therefore, from divine choice the laity have Christ for their brothers who though He is the Lord of all, came not to be served but to serve. They also have for their brothers those in the sacred ministry who by teaching, by sanctifying and by ruling with the authority of Christ feed the family of God so that the new commandment of charity may be fulfilled by all. St. Augustine puts this very beautifully when he says: "What I am for you terrifies me; what I am with you consoles me. For you I am a bishop; but with you I am a Christian. The former is a duty; the latter a grace. The former is a danger; the latter, salvation."

The laity are gathered together in the People of God and make up the Body of Christ under one head. Whoever they are they are called upon, as living members, to expend all their energy for the growth of the Church and its continuous sanctification, since this very energy is a gift of the Creator and a blessing of the Redeemer.

The lay apostolate, however, is a participation in the salvific mission of the Church itself. Through their baptism and confirmation all are commissioned to that apostolate by the Lord Himself. Moreover, by the sacraments, especially holy Eucharist, that charity toward God and man which is the soul of the apostolate is communicated and nourished. Now the laity are called in a special way to make the Church present and operative in those places and circumstances where only through them can it become the salt of the earth. Thus every layman, in virtue of the very gifts bestowed upon him, is at the same time a witness and a living instrument of the mission of the Church itself "according to the measure of Christ's bestowal."

Besides this apostolate which certainly pertains to all Christians, the laity can also be called in various ways to a more direct form of cooperation in the apostolate of the Hierarchy. This was the way certain men and women assisted Paul the Apostle in the Gospel, laboring much in the Lord. Further, they have the capacity to assume from the Hierarchy certain ecclesiastical functions, which are to be performed for a spiritual purpose.

Upon all the laity, therefore, rests the noble duty of working to extend the divine plan of salvation to all men of each epoch and in every land. Consequently, may every opportunity be given them so that, according to their abilities and the needs of the times, they may zealously participate in the saving work of the Church.

QUESTIONS FOR REVIEW

1. What is the "universal vocation"?
2. With each state in life, to whom is the person making a gift of themselves?
3. What are the gifts and fruits of the Holy Spirit?
4. What is your conscience and how does it guide you?
5. What are the different forms of prayer and what is the "perfect" prayer?

QUESTIONS FOR DISCUSSION

1. To what primary vocation do you believe God is calling you? Have you ever asked him what his will for you might be?
2. How can your life as a student or your work be a vocation? How should thinking of it as a vocation change how you approach these things?
3. Have you ever gone against your conscience? Explain. Why? How can you continue to form your conscience better for the future?

Appendix

CHALLENGES

"Sin," as we said in Part IV above, "makes you stupid." It prevents you from seeing your own sin and responding to truth. Sin, however, doesn't just make individuals "stupid." It also can make whole cultures "stupid." The farther the individuals within a culture move from God, the farther the culture as a whole moves. The laws that govern it—written and unwritten—become unbound from both the natural law and the divine law, and the people within it have a harder time recognizing the good, the true, and the beautiful.

This is the situation in which we find ourselves today in the West. As our culture has become unmoored from its Christian roots, people have lost their way. Not only do many people within the culture no longer understand the Church's teachings, but they have actually grown hostile to those teachings. They have grown hostile to Jesus, the Church, and virtue itself. Abortion, promiscuity, pornography, xenophobia, even greed are all often held up as "good" by our culture. Fidelity, chastity, self-sacrifice, and personal charity, on the other hand, are mocked. To live as a Catholic in this day and age is to live a countercultural life. It requires courage, wisdom, and perseverance. It also requires knowledge.

This book has aimed to give you as much knowledge as possible about the Church's moral teachings. In this appendix, we distill some of that knowledge in order to answer some of the most common objections you will likely face from others as you attempt to live your faith in the world.

If God Created Me to Be Free, Doesn't That Mean That I Alone Can Decide What Is Right and Wrong?

God did create you to be free, but not "free" in the sense that the postmodern world so often uses that word.

When the world today talks about freedom, it generally means freedom in the negative sense or "freedom from"—freedom from rules, freedom from authority, freedom from being told what to do. Some have described this notion of freedom as a freedom of indifference. It's a freedom with no purpose. It is indifferent, so to speak, in relation to any notion of good or right. This is the concept of freedom at the heart of modern Western culture, and it is often enshrined in liberal democracy, which sees freedom as the right to determine for ourselves what is good, right, and just, with no outside arbiter.

Freedom, when considered from this perspective, is diminished by anything that limits our options. This includes our natural inclinations, emotions, habits, traditions, families, relationships, and loyalties. In this conception of freedom, freedom itself becomes the highest good. Hence, the only real sin recognized by the modern world is to affect someone else in a way he does not want to be affected (to impose one's view on another by law or some other way).

Implicit in this notion of freedom is the idea that each person decides what is right or wrong. There can be no public morality or shared vision beyond the commitment to freedom itself. Reason, truth, and the law are also contrary to freedom in this conception. They limit options and coerce someone to make a certain decision over another. The only way to preserve freedom is thus to reject moral truth itself and limit law to preventing unwanted interactions. In short, modern society is relativist at its core, seeing all truth as "relative"—determined by individual experiences, situations, and opinions.

The Church, however, and most of historical Western society, has never thought this way about freedom or truth. In contrast to the culture's idea of a negative freedom or "freedom from," the Church has a positive vision of freedom. Freedom, for her, is always "freedom to"—freedom to love, freedom to serve, freedom to worship, freedom to be the people

God made us to be. In other words, freedom means being free to do the things God wants us to do without the constraints of sin holding us back.

According to this conception of freedom, we are free in this world because we can know the good, love the good, and choose the good—which aren't relative but fixed and unchanging, rooted in God himself and our own human nature. The more readily and easily we can know, love, and choose the good, the more free we are. Our judgments about the good and the readiness with which we act on those judgments help perfect us . . . and our freedom.

These two ways of looking at freedom could not be more different. According to the Church's understanding of freedom, the virtues develop freedom and perfect it since they are habits that allow us to choose the good easily, freely, and joyfully. We actually become more free when we have virtue. Virtues perfect the intellect and will according to their natural purposes, thereby bringing freedom itself to its perfection. To choose what is not good is an action against freedom, and makes us less free. A just law actually facilitates and aids our freedom by informing us what the good life is and what it is not. It thus guides and increases freedom. Here, what is important for the moral life is not autonomy or non-interference with others, but the truth.

None of this is true from a freedom of indifference perspective. In this way of seeing freedom, freedom is equally expressed no matter what we do. Bad choices don't limit freedom. Sin doesn't limit freedom. But virtues do. Laws do. Assertions of moral truth do. Thus, the capital sins in Western democracy are not pride, lust, or any of the other traditional sins, but rather coercion, dogmatism, and imposition.

And this brings us back to the original question: If God made us to be free, why can't we just decide for ourselves what is right and wrong? The answer is that God made us free to do what's right and avoid what's wrong. He gave us the freedom to do good and avoid evil—not to determine good and evil. We can't do that. He made us. He knows us better than we know ourselves. And he knows what will bring us the most joy, the most fulfillment, the most life. We can say no to his laws. We can say no to his guidance. But going against God's laws doesn't make them any less true, right, and good. In truth, when we say no to God's laws, we don't really break the laws; we break ourselves. We break our connection to the one who loves us and deny ourselves the very things we need to attain eternal joy.

Beyond that, to claim that any one person or individual gets to decide alone what is right and wrong is to deny the most fundamental truth about human nature: that we are made for communion, both with God and with each other. As the saying goes, "no man is an island." All that we know about right and wrong comes from our life in community. And all the choices we make about right and wrong have ramifications for the community. Our sins don't just hurt us; they hurt all the people around us. Adam's sin spilled over to affect every member of the human race. Our sins do something similar, if on a less grand scale. Think of all the people hurt by divorce, adultery, drug use, wastefulness, and even speeding. Sin has consequences that go well beyond the life of one individual, which is why no one person gets to be the ultimate arbiter of truth.

Virtue, however, works in a similar way. The good actions of Jesus Christ redeemed the people lost through Adam's sins. And the good actions of the saints redound through the ages. The saints used their God-given freedom not to define good, but to choose good. And all the world has benefitted from that choice.

Isn't It Wrong to Judge Other People by Telling Them Something They Are Doing Is Wrong?

Before we answer this question, let's step back for a minute and be honest with ourselves. Even though our culture has trained us to push back against any judgments of right and wrong, we all still judge others' actions a hundred times a day. Even the most hardened relativist does this. When someone cuts us off in traffic, we get angry at their reckless disregard for life and law. When someone is rude to us in a store, we're upset by their failure to treat us with respect. When we hear that someone is guilty of rape or murder, we don't think, "Who am I to judge?" No! We think, "That's wrong!" Even when someone judges us harshly and we push back against their judgment, we're doing the very thing we're telling them they shouldn't do: we're making a judgment about their behavior.

The truth is, judgment of actions is essential for the good life and for charity. We must judge what is good and evil, otherwise we can't choose one and avoid the other. Every action we do (whether we like it or not) presupposes some judgment of good and evil.

Likewise, we can't love someone, at least not authentically, if we don't judge good and evil. Love presupposes the truth. If we want to will the good for another person, what we will for them must be authentically good. In the modern world, we have confused love for support, thinking loving someone requires we support whatever decisions people make for their life. Nobody wants to follow this line of thought to its logical conclusion, though, which would entail supporting *every* possible decision someone could make, from self-starvation to self-mutilation, drug abuse, and worse.

Most of us know that supporting those decisions isn't loving at all. If we love someone, we don't want them to harm themselves. But the spiritual harm inflicted by sin is even worse than the physical harm inflicted by self-starvation. Sin separates us from God and can endanger our souls forever, for all eternity. If you love someone, you can't support their decision to kill themselves spiritually any more than you can support their decision to use heroin.

It also helps to remember that sin doesn't just hurt the sinner. Sin has social consequences. Some of those consequences are easy to see. Murder, rape, and theft have obvious victims. Adultery, fornication, apostasy, lying, racism, detraction, and all the other sins we discussed in Part II have victims too. Sin harms both perpetrator and victim, so loving others demands judgment. It demands that we try to work against decisions that will hurt individuals, families, and entire cultures.

If we really want what is best for others, then, yes, at times, we must be willing to do the hard thing and correct them. We must be willing to try to stop them from doing something bad and bringing harm upon themselves and others. Authentic love cannot desire or work for what is bad. That's hatred, the very opposite of love. So, if we love each other, we must encourage each other to live a life free of sin, a life of true happiness. It is actually a sin of omission to fail to correct another (if you think the correction will prevent the sin). God calls us to love the sinner and hate the sin. In fact, the reason we hate the sin is because we love the sinner. We want the good for them, not the evil. That is the very core of love.

In effect, the modern world's rejection of sin is a rejection of love itself and what it implies for human relationships. You do not love and cannot love unless you have a sense of the truth and what negates it (sin). The "live and let live" mentality is not so much a benign social lubricant as it is hatred and indifference for others. These are the opposite of the virtue of charity, the opposite of the good life to which we are called in Christ.

All that being said, however, there is a time and place for fraternal correction. For example, walking up to a person you don't know at Mass and telling them they're dressed inappropriately is a bad idea. They might be dressed inappropriately, but chances are it's not your place to tell them that. Correcting strangers' behavior in an insensitive and imprudent way is wrong. Correcting anyone's behavior in an insensitive and imprudent way is wrong. If we're going to correct someone, we need to be sensitive to the time and place we do it, the relationship we have with the person, and most of all, how we do it. Charity must always come first. Just because someone else is doing something wrong doesn't give us license to be rude, inappropriate, or cruel.

Along similar lines, we need to remember that there is a difference between judging actions and judging people. Unless you're God, you can't accurately judge the interior state of another human being. You can't know how or why they make the decisions they do. You can't fully judge their knowledge, freedom, and culpability. Nor can you necessarily judge their intentions. Only God can do that.

Remember how we talked about the sin of rash judgment in Part II? That's what we need to avoid here, as well. We should always presuppose the best about others and their motives until we are forced to do otherwise by the evidence. Much of what we reject today as unjust judgment is actually rash judgment, but we lack the vocabulary to name it correctly.

Likewise, there are certain situations in which fraternal correction would not be loving and should not be done. This is especially when it will not make a difference and will actually harm the relationship. Oftentimes those who are fraternally corrected, especially if they lack the virtue of docility, will rebel even further in response and cut off all possibilities of further dialogue. In these cases, the evil action is to be tolerated but not condoned or facilitated. Tolerance, in its authentic meaning, is the response of a person who permits an evil to exist for a good reason (because it cannot be eradicated at all or not right now) or its eradication would do more harm than good. Tolerance does not approve, celebrate, or facilitate evil.

Isn't It Wrong for the Church to Impose Her Views of Morality on Others?

This objection is just another version of the first two. Because Western liberal democracy is founded on the principle that each person has the right to define the good life for himself, the attempts of anyone who tries to answer that question for us, much less make us act in accord with their vision, often is seen as an unjust imposition that thwarts our fundamental rights.

That reaction, however, isn't in accord with reality. Someone is always making rules that others have to live by. Rules about what speed we drive, what taxes we pay, what guns we can buy, what medical research is permissible, what property rights apply to individuals, who is allowed to enter the country, and millions of other such rules are imposed on us every day. They have to be. If not, we would live in a state of absolute anarchy. In order to keep the peace, order society, and promote the common good, some form of morality will always be imposed on us. And that morality doesn't just fall from the sky. It is rooted in someone's vision of the good life.

Like it or not, someone is going to be imposing their morality on us. But it's not just the lawmakers who impose their beliefs on us. We do the same to others. Every activity we undertake changes the possible options for the people around us. When we choose to stop at a yellow light, we force those behind us to wait. When we are in charge of a business and set hours for opening and closing, we limit the freedom of our workers to come and go at their leisure. We also limit the freedom of our clients to avail themselves of our services whenever they like.

Imposition via activity is simply unavoidable. Imposition via law is also unavoidable. It's the only way we can live in society with each other. But, when we remember how the Church understands freedom—in a positive way, where we are free to be the people God made us to be, unencumbered by sin—imposition in the above scenarios is not a problem at all as long as it's grounded in the truth. In fact, it's a good thing to impose and enforce good laws. Who wants a society in which murder is legal? Who wants to live in a culture where no one ever obeys the traffic laws?

We are social animals, and our perfection comes about through living in society. Speed limits teach us patience. Anti-littering laws teach us stewardship. Laws that prohibit stealing teach us to respect private property. Good laws help us to act with virtue. They both teach and reinforce good behavior. The imposition of activity is only problematic if it is based on a false conception of the human person and society, that is to say, if it's not based on the natural law.

This brings us back to the original question, which somewhat misses the point. Although our government imposes beliefs on us all the time, the Church doesn't impose anything on anyone who is not a part of the Church. The Church proclaims the truth of Jesus Christ as revealed through Scripture and Tradition. She articulates the natural law and the divine law. People are then free to believe what the Church proclaims and articulates or not. They're free to conform their lives to reality or not. The Church doesn't force anyone to believe the truth and live in accord with it. She is the "pillar and bulwark of the truth" (1 Tim 3:15) to whom Jesus entrusted the responsibility of teaching everyone what God has revealed about the good life. Teaching, however, is not the same as imposing. Teaching is a proposition. The Church calls to the world and invites it to follow the truth, but she doesn't force anyone to answer that invitation.

What about when the Church lobbies for certain laws, though? Is not that an unjust imposition? No. That's just the Church proclaiming the truth in the public square. That's the Church trying to help all people recognize the demands of the natural law, which, remember, is binding on all people. We were all made to live in accord with natural law. It's the law that shows human beings how to live. The Church has a responsibility to all people. She wants all people to live in accord with truth, and making the case for that truth is both her duty and her right.

The same applies to individual believers. Like all citizens in a representative democracy, we have a right to lobby for laws that reflect what we believe is right and true. Even more than that, because our beliefs are shaped by the Church and rooted in the truth of Christ, we have an obligation to lobby for civil laws that reflect the truth of the natural law. Remember, laws help people to grow in virtue. So, of course we want our country, state, and local community to have laws that will do that.

At the same time, just because we know the truth doesn't mean we *always* should impose it via law. Sometimes, outlawing certain activities or promoting others (even if the activities in question are truly evil or good) can do more harm than good in society. Consider, for example, the Church's teachings on fornication. Both the natural law and divine law teach us that fornication is wrong. The Church, however, isn't interested in making fornication illegal. She has discerned that civil laws, which have sought to do that, do more harm than good. So, she continues to proclaim the eternal consequences of fornication, but she doesn't try to convince the government to impose any legal consequences on the act. Like the Church, individual Christians have to make similar judgment calls about what laws we propose and support. Truth is central and necessary, but we also must have political prudence to know when to impose the truth and when to tolerate evil.

Why Can't We Make up Our Own Minds and Be in Control of Everything?

Did you make the sun rise this morning? Do you control the oceans tides? Do you know the mind and heart of every single human being—past, future, and present?

Easy answer: No.

This is why we cannot be in control of everything. Because we are finite. We are creatures. We have limits. There are no ifs, ands, or buts about that. We did not choose to be born, let alone be born in this time, this place, or to our parents. Forget the desire to control everything: there is hardly anything we can control. Most of us can barely manage to get out of the house on time, with all the things we need each day, let alone control "everything" in the entire universe.

The truth is, humanity isn't much good at controlling things. Look at our national debt. Look at government bureaucracy, red tape, and inefficiency. Look the economic inequality and serious poverty of much of the world. Look at the World War I, the Nazi Holocaust, and the ongoing terrorist attacks of radical Islam. For the most part, when humanity is put in charge of things, we screw it up.

This is why, for all of us, one of the best, most important (and hardest) things we will ever do is recognize that we are not in control. That's God's job and God's alone. Acknowledging this requires humility. It requires acknowledging our total dependence on God. It requires recognizing our own limitations. But it's really the only way. We can't always know or understand God's ways, but we can trust that they are the best, even if it doesn't seem so at first. God loves us so much that he died on the Cross for us. He loves us so much that he takes on the appearance of bread and wine and feeds us with his own Body in the Eucharist every day. He knows more than us, he sees more than us, and he loves more than us. He really does know what he is doing, and he has shown us that we can trust him. Our job is simply to do that.

At the same time, though, we don't *have to* trust God. God lets us make up our own minds about what we believe and don't believe. He allows us to follow our conscience . . . even if our conscience leads us straight to hell. Of course, he wants us to take the time to form our conscience. He wants us to see reality as it really is and know the truth. But still, he doesn't force us to do that. Neither does the Church. The Church proclaims the truth and is the means by which we can receive the grace we need to hear and understand the truth, but the choice to receive that grace and act on it is up to us. The choice to believe is up to us.

None of the Church's members on earth are perfect. We all have sinned. But the Church herself remains the Body and Bride of Christ, who has been empowered by Jesus to continue his mission. He speaks through her. He acts through her. He applies the graces he won for us on the Cross through her. Obedience isn't our only choice, but given all Jesus has done for us, it's the only choice that makes sense. Ultimately, our sinfulness can only be overcome by Christ's salvation, the salvation that comes in and through the Church. We cannot save ourselves or earn God's grace. Nor can we make the perfect society here on earth. Humanity can't perfect itself. Humanity can't save itself. Only Christ can do that. All comes as a gift. Having the humility to recognize this is a great grace and key to the life of true freedom.

There's an Old Saying about Charity Beginning at Home. Doesn't This Mean That I Don't Have to Worry about Helping Anyone Else until I Have Enough to Take Care of My Family and Myself?

It's true that the virtue of charity has an order. We can equally will the good for all people, but we can't act out of that love equally for all people. That would be impossible. We are finite creatures. We've only got so much time and energy to give. So, we have to discern how to proportion both out while still following the second greatest commandment. To help us with this, the Church proposes an order to charity.

In that order, our families do hold a primary place. Family is the first school of virtue. It is where we learn how to live authentic charity. We are bound to our family by place, time, opportunity, and blood. Accordingly, family comes first.

Once our obligations to our family are met, however, we then have an obligation to the other people who immediately surround us: our neighbors, co-workers, and friends. We can't give them the time and devotion that we give to our families, but we still need to do what we can to meet their needs and help them in times of difficulty.

Then, there are the people God sends our way each day: the homeless person on the street, the clerk in the grocery store, the stranger on the internet in need of a kind word. We're called to help them to the degree we are able, even if it's only with a $5 bill, a smile, or a word of encouragement.

Beyond that, we're called to give what we can and do what we can help to people in need beyond our sphere of influence—supporting apostolates that work with the poor or women in crisis pregnancies, missionaries in foreign lands, or political groups advocating for just causes.

That help might not be much; maybe the most we can give is our prayers. But some help we must give.

We can't work for everyone's good equally. And yet, while each of us has to discern how to divide up our time and energy based on our various vocations and states in life, we still have to love everyone. Charity has to animate our every thought about them and our every action towards them. Anything less would adulterate the Gospel. Anything less would eviscerate the Christian life, which is a life of loving sacrifice in service of God and neighbor.